Who Am I?

How Do I Find Me?

With high chopes
and best wishes
on the road to
self discovery!

Who Am I?

How Do I Find Me?

by
Meda Killgore

The case histories and individuals discussed throughout this text are based on the lives of real people. The names and life circumstances have been dramatically altered to protect the identity and confidentiality of these individuals.

First printing: 2008

Cover photo: www.kevinthom.com

Cover design: Cody Killgore
Website design: Neill Killgore

Table of Contents

An in-the-moment, self-preserving strategy
Speaking our truths about others, to them
Speaking our truths to heal and empower the true self
Exercise

Forgiving others
Strengthening our compassionate response
Cultural compassion
Forgiving ourselves
Dealing with guilt
Deliberate forgiveness
Benefits of forgiveness
Forgiveness and how to heal and empower the true self
Exercise

Acknowledgements

I owe a heartfelt debt of gratitude to my husband, Chris. His belief in me has been my anchor in times of doubt and indecision. Chris' *why-not* attitude has challenged me to face many fears and to manifest my dreams. Without his support, this book would not exist. Chris played a major role in helping me create the time and space I needed to write. His encouragement never wavered. *Thank you, Chris for your friendship, your love, your wisdom and your ongoing support.*

I would like to thank my sons, Neill and Cody. Neill spent an enormous amount of time learning the Flash software to create my website and to keep it updated. Cody performed magic with software as he worked with Kevin Thom's photo to create the book cover design. Somehow, both Neill and Cody managed to transform my non-technical requests (*friendly font, no sharp edges, no angry colors*) into the reality of a beautiful website (www.medakillgore.com) and book cover. *Thank you, Neill and Cody for your talents and willingness to be of assistance.*

I am very grateful to my brother, Bill King (www.positract.com), for his steadfast belief in me. His unconditional acceptance of my ideas and his willingness to test the techniques has been greatly appreciated. Billy also spent significant time editing and offering feedback on content. *Thank you, Billy.*

Thanks are also in order for Rose Daigle. Her gentle but persistent nudges to get this book on paper have kept the project moving. Rose, a retired sociology professor and licensed professional counselor, contributed invaluable knowledge and emotional support whenever called upon. *Thank you, Rose.*

Thanks to John and Betty King, my mom and dad, for the sacrifices they made on behalf of me and my five siblings. Those sacrifices insured a top notch education in spite of multiple moves in the early years of our lives. Mom's belief in me has been like a ray of sunshine on a dark night. I have called on mom many times for encouragement to keep this project alive. Her message is constant: *Meda, people need to hear what you have to say. You can make a difference in a lot of people's lives. Get that book written.* Thank you, Mom. Thank you, Dad.

To my sister, Rita, who for as long as I can remember, set a high standard of excellence. I have no doubt that my goal *to be just like my sister* has served me well. *Thank you, Rita.*

A sincere thank you goes to Diane Zimberoff and David Hartman of the Wellness Institute, Seattle, WA, (www.wellnessinstitute.org) for their contribution to my overall knowledge with regard to the workings of the unconscious. The two years of hypnotherapy training I received from Wellness played a significant role in putting my own personal healing on a fast track. With Dianne and David's encouragement, I have learned the importance of accessing repressed memories and working within those memories to secure healing outcomes. With their guidance, I have gained the skills to put this knowledge to work. *Thank you, Diane and David.*

Sharon Shane (www.sharonshane.com) gave me my first lesson in dream interpretation. She turned me on to the wisdom of dreams and I've never looked back. Sharon also gave me the vocabulary and the know-how to challenge the workings of the negative ego in my life. *Thank you, Sharon.*

The editors of Two Brothers Press (www.twobrotherspress. net) have helped me immeasurably. Their knowledge and vision have contributed significantly to the rhythm and readability of this volume. Due to their assistance, I have been rescued from pronoun chaos, carried through comma confusion and empowered with kind words of correction and encouragement. Their genuine interest and enthusiasm as well as their willingness to go the extra mile has been evident throughout their communications. *Thank you, Ron and John!*

Kevin Thom, the incredible photographer who captured the essence of this book in his single photo entitled *Chameleon,* has supported me from that first contact two years ago. At that time, he graciously agreed to the use of one of his photos on my website. Now, he has allowed the use of *Chameleon* for the cover. I can attest to Kevin's generosity of spirit. The images on his website (www. kevinthom.com) speak for the range of his talent. *Thank you, Kevin.*

I am immensely grateful to my clients, *Joey, Celeste and Grace* for allowing me to include their stories in this book. It is my hope that their incredible courage and perseverance has shown through the necessary camouflage of their identities. *Thank you, Joey, Celeste and Grace for the honor of working with you and witnessing your enormous strength as you moved toward greater expression of your True Self.*

I am indebted to the following for their role in helping this book come to fruition. These individuals have contributed directly and indirectly to the creation of this book. Thank you!

Charles and Patti Killgore
Rick Emerson
Henry Hamilton
Donna Voll
Julia Muir
Jo Kornegay Downey
Cathy Geniti
Sherry O'Brian
Aleyda Martinez Novotny
John C. King, Jr.
Robert King
Tom King
All my Wellness friends

And, finally, I owe a substantial debt of gratitude to *Lauren* for pausing in the midst of her deep personal pain to look me in the eye and say earnestly:

Ms. Meda, you need to write a book!

In loving memory

of

Dorothy Bendey

Ina King

Maggie Gau

Introduction

At the very beginning of my counseling career, I had the good fortune of meeting six different women with the exact same complaint. These women came from different economic, social, and ethnic backgrounds. Their ages were somewhat similar, i.e., they were all between thirty-five and forty-five. Each woman was very, very depressed and could give no explanation for their sad feelings. They could detail for me their successes. They were excellent employees, mothers, wives, sisters, daughters, Sunday school teachers, etc., but each one of them had neglected one very important person in her life – herself! Without fail, as each came to recognize and accept that happiness required embracing and nurturing herself, they all had the same two questions: *Who am I? How do I find me?*

From there, the stories differ because of each woman's uniqueness and experiences. Meeting and working with those women helped me recognize early in my career that there is a part of each of us that longs for expression, that nudges us intuitively, that speaks to us in the form of dreams, that grabs our attention with physical symptoms, and that *will not be repressed*. I call that part in each of us the true self. I believe it is the *true* self because I have witnessed depression lift, anxiety fade, and lives be transformed as a result of listening to its messages.

In this book, I share the stories of a few clients, detailing their struggles and triumphs as they work to get back in touch with their true natures. I share a few personal stories as well – as I could not help others if I had not also done the work myself.

This book is broken down into three sections. In Part One, I discuss how the true self gets lost. In Part Two, I share strategies for recognizing and connecting with the true self. Finally, in Part Three, I share specific techniques for how to heal and empower the self.

When I met those six women, I had no idea how their common but complex problems would help me with my future clients or my own personal quest. I am eternally grateful to those women and every client who has ever walked through my office door. Their willingness to be vulnerable is a huge but necessary step on the road to the true self.

It is with deep humility that I offer these ideas for your consideration. Some ideas will open an avenue of healing for you. Others may not appeal to you. Trust what interests you as the path to choose for a while. This is not a comprehensive volume. It won't address everyone's issues. But if you walk away from this book with just one self-discovery strategy in hand, you'll be taking that important first step on your road to self-empowerment.

Meda

By the way, it was merely coincidental that those clients were women. Since then, I have met countless men in similar circumstances!

Part One

As we move through life, we make countless decisions about how to be and who we are. Within those decisions, likely to be long forgotten, lie discarded longings and unexpressed, undeveloped aspects of the true self. Many of those discarded aspects of ourselves can be found in our childhoods. Others may have been left behind only yesterday. As part of our quest to connect with our true selves, an essential step is to identify and affirm these aspects.

In Part One, we take a glimpse at three important areas of influence: our childhood experiences, the culture we live in, and the negative ego that resides within our psyches. These have likely influenced us in countless positive ways. The focus, by necessity, is on the negative experiences, because it is within those experiences that we learn to compromise ourselves by deferring to others.

The goal of this section is to get you thinking about your life and how your negative experiences may still be in your present moment. As you read through the information, have a notebook nearby. The ideas and client stories may trigger thoughts of some of your own experiences. Write those down so that you can work with them as you progress through the book.

We plan our lives according to a dream that came to us in our childhood, and we find that life alters our plans.

—Ben Okri

Chapter 1 - Childhood and the Self

We spend a lot of time as children, scattering parts of our true selves to the four corners of the world. By the time we're adults, we've forgotten where those pieces and parts lie, yet we sense that something is missing. We long be whole, to find those missing pieces, but we no longer have ready access to the faces and places of our childhoods.

We're very psychologically vulnerable as children. Sure, we're all born unique and with a vast array of potential. But if our parents are wounded by the experiences of their lives, they may not know how to nurture us in the ways that we need. The result is that we end up reenacting our parents' wounds, unaware that we're doing it. Or if we are aware, we sure don't know how to change it.

People who come to counseling often say that they don't want to dredge up childhood issues, that they want to deal with the problem at hand. I usually assure them that I, too, prefer to work in the present. True and lasting progress is dependent, however, on working with core issues, not just their symptoms. Childhood issues, along with the need to reclaim those lost parts of ourselves, are at the core of many of our present-moment problems.

At life's beginning just moments from the womb, we begin to define ourselves by our parents' reactions to us. A parent's eyes can mirror back to us our beauty and worth. Those of us who are lucky enough to have experienced that loving and expressive *twinkle* in the eye of the beholder know exactly how empowering and welcoming it feels. What if the parent's eyes are clouded with issues of survival, illness, addiction, or personal crisis? Not yet emotionally developed or cognitively capable of understanding, we're at risk to sense rejection and to search for the meaning of that rejection. Often, we turn against ourselves, believing that we're defective, and therein lies the first of many potentially long-lasting and damaging identity decisions. Such decisions hold the potential for permanent separation from the true self.

The search for, and discovery of those old decisions holds the promise of wholeness and reconciliation with those old discarded parts of ourselves. The purpose of this chapter is not to bash or criticize our parents. Instead, the purpose is to encourage a look into childhood for potential wounds that maybe, in some way, have had an impact on your present moment in a negative way. If you do find something that can be corrected, you have something tangible with which to work. Beginning with Chapter Four, you are given strategies for dealing with anything that you might find.

Childhood decisions

Three areas of adult functioning that are dramatically shaped by our childhood experiences are:

1.   how we develop our self-concept
2.   how we interact within relationships
3.   how we cope with problems

These three areas are the most common places where my clients find negative material related to their childhoods. We will be focusing on these three areas within each chapter throughout this book.

Self-concept

Our self-concepts can be defined as the ideas or mental images we have of ourselves. These images become more complex as we get older and add more traits. As children, we begin by interpreting the feedback we get from others. Although we *do* have a choice of internalizing that feedback or rejecting it, unfortunately, the younger we are, the more likely it is that we will accept without question and internalize such feedback. We also look to our parents for self-concept clues. For example, if our parents repeatedly comment on their fat bodies or their poor health, we as children take a look at our bodies and begin to define ourselves as fat or not fat and healthy or not healthy. In a sense, it's as though our parents teach us our self-concept priorities. Our siblings, peers, and other adults gain more influence over us as we grow older. Sometimes, their relationships with us can erase some old, faulty beliefs but, at other times, we validate old ones or gain new ones.

Our level of sensitivity can contribute to our self-concept by making us more (or less) vulnerable to others in our world. Our uniqueness includes a level of sensitivity that varies dramatically within families and across cultures. Children within the same family will experience the same parenting style in different ways. One child might be predictably compliant while the other rebels, resisting every form of control and discipline. Likewise, a harsh parental tone will go unnoticed by one child, while another child will notice it, give it meaning and adjust his or her reactions and behaviors because of it. If we're highly sensitive, we're at higher risk to take on another's opinion of us. If we are highly insensitive, we risk ignoring important feedback from others. In either case, we risk never really developing our own unique and healthy self-concept.

Our self-concept is at the mercy of many, many variables, known and unknown. For example, children who suffer from injustices like neglect or abuse rarely afford themselves the luxury of connecting with the true self. Instead, with *safety* and *being loved* as overriding core needs, a child tends to assess others for how to react and how to be. Deferring to others in this manner is a form of abandonment, i.e., self-abandonment.

Don't panic, thinking you have to examine every self-concept decision you ever made about yourself. The important ideas that need to be challenged will come to the surface as you work through the remainder of this book.

Relationships

Our experiences growing up also result in decisions about how to interact with others. If our parents are timid and passive with others, we might reach adulthood believing that that is the way to be. If our parents are disrespectful to others, we are at risk to be disrespectful too! If our parents use stereotypes and are prejudiced, we might catch ourselves being that as well. We do have choices about our decisions, but there is risk created when negative elements are present. The risk involves reenacting the same behavior we saw growing up or reacting to it by becoming the extreme opposite. In other words, in addition to being at risk to make a childhood decision to be timid and passive, there is also risk to decide to be overly bold and aggressive. Regardless, our behavior and personality choices are generally made based on what we have witnessed.

It is in our closest relationships that repressed childhood issues come to light. We might, for example, catch ourselves using words and ideas that we heard our parents use. Or we may note patterns in our relationships that were also in our parents' relationships.

Based on my observations within therapy, we tend to draw people and events into our lives that reflect our unfinished business. It's as though we recreate specific scenes and themes from our childhood. I recall a parent who came for counseling because she had disciplined her child by giving her a spanking. The situation did not involve abuse at all. But the woman was concerned because, as a child, she swore she would never strike her children. I asked her the age of her child. She replied "Six." I then asked how old she was when her mother had first struck her. She replied "Six." I have heard this type of history-repeating scenario over and over again. The good news is that a pattern can be changed once it is identified.

In later chapters, we will take a closer look at personal relationships with an eye on identifying your personal risk areas. For now, if you have questions or observations about your past, make a note of them. Odds are that, by the end of the book, you will have utilized the information to chart a course in the search for your true self.

Coping

Finally, it should come as no surprise to hear that how we cope with problems is largely based on how we have observed others doing so. Our coping style is found within our ability to face responsibilities and challenges. Growing up, we observed the adults in our lives and how they dealt with life's challenges. Some may have chosen healthy means to cope while others turned to substances, like drugs and alcohol, when things got tough. Common, unhealthy coping styles we may have observed while growing up include denial, rationalization, repression, acting out, etc.

An example of a common problematic coping skill that I have observed within counseling involves handling conflict. When asked how their parents handled conflict, these clients answer that their parents never argued or they fought all the time. The clients in these cases never learned how to handle conflict in a healthy way. Another interesting observation is that many of these clients do a great job with conflict at work, but in their most intimate relationships (spouse, children, etc.) they have problems.

The bottom line is that we *do* make lasting coping decisions while growing up. Those decisions may or may not serve us very well. Examining the coping styles of the significant adults from each of our pasts and comparing them to each of our coping styles in the present is an important step to making present-moment, conscious decisions.

Joey and Celeste

I'd like to introduce you to Joey and Celeste—two separate stories of two very opposite clients that illustrate many childhood challenges. As you read about Joey and Celeste, assess their self-concept, consider their beliefs about relationships, and finally, examine their coping skills.

Joey's Story – *A story of neglect, and emotional and physical abuse*

Joey came to counseling because of a deep, paralyzing depression. He was very lonely and saw no reason to hope that his situation would improve. As I observed and listened to Joey that first day, I couldn't help but notice the extreme anger that accompanied nearly every problem that he related to me. Joey was angry with his ex-wife, his mother, his boss, his co-workers and, it seemed, anyone with whom he had more than a casual acquaintance. He was unhappy at work, unhappy at home, and unhappy with himself. Joey used language and phrases that I might be more likely to hear from a child. In that first session, he used statements like: *It's not fair, She made me do it, He was mean to me.* These statements were my first clues that Joey's childhood contained a host of unresolved hurts and grievances.

The facts that eventually unfolded were that Joey had been emotionally abused and neglected most of his childhood. He endured at least two occasions of extreme physical abuse. Joey was the family scapegoat. His father berated him often and unfairly. His mother never sided with him or spoke up for him. Joey's brothers were older and had lots of problems. When things went wrong in the family, it would somehow end up being Joey's fault. Joey was very sensitive and would cry easily, which only made matters worse. His entire family would mimic and ridicule him when he was emotional. His brothers would blame him for things they had done, and Joey's parents always believed his brothers. Never did they listen to him. When Joey's brothers played sports, his parents were always in attendance. When Joey played, they rarely came. And, if they did come, he got to hear about his mistakes when it was over. At school, Joey was so inhibited that he did not even try to make friends. He decided to become invisible to others and apparently succeeded. Joey's childhood was devoid of any gestures of love. He spent his childhood being ignored, blamed, cursed, punished, and humiliated. The one bright spot for Joey was that he did well at school. Joey could look at his grades and feel good about getting A's and B's because that meant he was "Excellent" or "Above Average."

When Joey graduated from high school, he decided to attend a college that was sufficiently far from home that he would not be expected to visit often. He had earned scholarships that provided tuition, room and board, and even some spending money. Joey continued his pattern of trying to be invisible to others, but as fate would have it, one young lady did notice him. She was relentless in her pursuit, ignoring his distancing tactics. Joey became intrigued in this young lady's attraction to him. Once he allowed himself to engage in conversation with her, a courtship began. It wasn't long before Joey fell hopelessly in love. Never in his life had someone wanted to be with him. Never in his life had someone given him a compliment. Joey couldn't ask her to marry him fast enough! After all, here was someone who saw value in him. This was a new experience for Joey. He wanted to hang onto this girl and never let go. So, Joey was married by the time he was nineteen.

Initially, Joey was very happy. He relished the time with his wife. He lavished her with attention and was genuinely kind to her. Unfortunately, the story does not have a happy ending. Neither Joey nor his new wife were prepared for the emotional challenges of intimacy. Both were students. Both worked part-time jobs to support themselves through school. The financial pressures resulted in lots of arguments, and Joey's only experience with how to handle disagreement was that which he had seen growing up. Their conflict was filled with blame, shouting, and threats. At the end of each disagreement, Joey would distance himself (exactly as he had as a child). His wife would plead with him to talk to her, but Joey learned at an early age not to express his true feelings. As the wall of silence grew larger and more ominous, Joey's wife grew more and more unhappy. Her unhappiness fed Joey's self-doubt and feelings of defectiveness. Three years later, both miserable, they agreed to a divorce that became final one month after graduation.

I didn't meet Joey until he was thirty-five. He had never remarried. It was painfully clear in that first session, that before Joey could ever be happily married, there was one important relationship that needed nurturing—and that was his relationship with himself. Over the course of his years at home, Joey learned to believe that he was faulty and defective. He believed he did not deserve to be loved. He doubted that anyone could like him, and he looked for evidence to support his negative beliefs. In a psychological sense, Joey ended up recreating the emotional abuse by berating himself with his negative self-talk (verbal abuse). Joey's true self was effectively imprisoned, trapped in childhood, and not allowed to risk intimacy or growth. He couldn't permit himself to trust that someone would care about him, as this meant eventual conflict and pain. If I were Joey's Self, I'd be depressed and angry too!

Joey's eventual self-rescue took several years. The road to his success was blocked often by self-doubt and indecision. Despite numerous stumbling blocks, Joey kept stepping up to the plate. Joey's true self had an incredible will to live and to be expressed. Every time I thought those strong emotions of anger and depression were about to negate his progress, he managed to pull himself up by his bootstraps and begin again. I came to admire Joey for his courage and perseverance in the face of many challenges.

Imagine what it would be like to be Joey. His only experiences with loved ones involved abuse and neglect. Is it any wonder that as Joey dared to experiment with intimacy, he would have had problems? Joey's childhood-influenced *self-concept* consisted of beliefs of inferiority and inadequacy. His childhood experiences caused him to believe that in close relationships, people were often neglectful and harbored critical thoughts about each other. This drastically affected his *relationship* with his wife who quickly grew tired of her words and motives being twisted and questioned. Their relationship began to mimic that of his parents. There was a lot of conflict. Joey had two *coping styles* that were brought forward from childhood. Initially, he would withdraw into self-blame and distance himself from his wife. From that vantage point, he grew resentful and would begin to look outward for evidence of others fault. After a while, he would become so angry, he would begin to accuse his wife of all kinds of hurtful and neglectful acts—most of which he manufactured within his own pain. When Joey was finally able to perceive through the eyes of the adult, he saw clearly that he had been neglectful and abusive, that he was recreating the dynamics in his parents' relationship. But, it wasn't all Joey's fault! It takes two to have a relationship. Both he and his wife had brought to the marriage the best coping mechanisms they had learned. They simply were not equipped with the awareness and the tools needed to develop new, more effective means of coping.

Fortunately for Joey, he made a decision after the first session to make changes in his life. His plan, by necessity, included self-discovery and self-empowerment. To do so, he worked to expand his awareness to include how his past experiences were contributing to the present problems in his life. The awareness grew quickly. Changing the patterns was more difficult. Joey left counseling more prepared to walk in the present moment and more prepared to recognize that many of his negative feelings and automatic coping mechanisms were associated with his childhood experiences—not with his true self.

Celeste's story – *a story of overindulgence*

Celeste was twenty-eight when I met her. She had a great personality, complemented by her natural beauty and ready smile. Those traits had served her well in her budding career as a marketing representative for a national company, but she had not been able to have success in her relationships with men. Celeste was married at twenty-five and divorced at twenty-six. Her marriage to a physically abusive man lasted three months. Celeste wanted to have success in matters of love but she said she needed help. She knew that she had a pattern and she wanted it to stop.

Celeste's pattern went something like this: Celeste would meet and begin dating someone whom she perceived as being *perfect* for her. In the throes of infatuation, Celeste gathered convincing evidence to support the idea that this someone was *the man of her dreams*. In the meantime, the man whose self-image was bolstered by the fact that someone as beautiful as Celeste could love him fell head over heels into infatuation with her also. The man would go to great lengths to please Celeste. She got flowers, compliments, notes, and a seemingly inexhaustible supply of words of love. Most notably, Celeste got her man's *undivided attention*. Within a week of meeting each other, the two spent every possible waking moment together. No relationship can sustain this level of intensity for long. As soon as Celeste's man would start to move toward a more balanced relationship, like wanting a night apart, Celeste would launch into a rage of jealousy. She challenged any effort he made toward balance with a charge of not wanting her. The more this situation repeated itself, the more unattractive Celeste became to her man. In the end, he broke up with her, *but* it took numerous attempts because each effort to detach was met by an even sweeter Celeste who promised to change.

In the end, Celeste was dumped. Because Celeste was so attractive, it wasn't long before she met another *perfect* man. And, interestingly, it was part of her pattern that she could now tell someone everything that was wrong with the first man and why the relationship was not destined to be. It was as if she was wearing blinders in the courtship phase and using a microscope after the breakup.

It was abundantly evident during the first session (and every session thereafter) that Celeste could only love herself if someone else loved her. She had an insatiable appetite for attention. There seemed to be no internal base of self-support to build upon.

Working with Celeste was not easy. She would disappear from counseling for months or years at a time. She seemed to want to change but she could not stop repeating the pattern. When she finally decided that she should take a break from dating while she explored her issues in counseling, she got very depressed. It was as if without someone, she was nothing. She put herself down. She talked about being desperately lonely. After about two weeks of depression and loneliness, Celeste would either find a new boyfriend or contact an old one. Celeste was locked into a pattern with no obvious way out.

How could this have happened? Celeste was obviously intelligent, successful, creative, and beautiful. Although it was clear that the issues that supported Celeste's pattern related to primary relationships, problems leading to her issue were not as apparent as Joey's.

Clues began to emerge as Celeste discussed her *perfect* childhood. She was welcomed into the world by a doting mother and father. She was a beautiful baby. From the start, Celeste exhibited a genuine and warm personality, traits that attracted others. She was an only child. She could do no wrong. Her parents planned their lives around her needs. Everyone, including grandparents and neighbors, loved to be around Celeste. As she grew, Celeste got everything she wanted. No one could deny such a sweet child anything. Is it any wonder, then, that Celeste would expect the world to treat her as special? From her point of view, all she ever experienced from others was admiration and acceptance. Because Celeste got so much worth from the outside world, she never had to develop her own internal sense of worth. Her only measure was what other people thought of her. Celeste's desperation (when dumped) made more sense when I realized how dependent she was on others for her sense of worth.

The only way out for Celeste was to learn how to value and express her true self without giving too much consideration to what others thought of her. Ultimately, in order to allow this to happen, Celeste had to stop asking for others' opinions and approval in their words and actions. She had to begin to look within, to discover and empower her self without any help from others. This would prove to be Celeste's greatest challenge.

Celeste's childhood-influenced *self-concept* was built completely on the opinions of others. She had no base of self-support for times when things went wrong in her life. She needed to have someone in her life as a source of identity. In *relationships*, others were expected to dote on her, overlook faults, and not bring up problems. And, finally, Celeste's adult *coping style* was a direct result of her childhood. When there was a problem, she expected people to listen to her and be charmed by her ideas. If this did not work, she might get angry and demand agreement. But, in the end, she was so tied to others' opinions and approval, she would become desperate. The result was that she coped by changing herself and her needs in an effort to smooth over the problem and sustain the relationship.

In summary, throughout Celeste's life, people lavished an extraordinary amount of attention upon her. She was given everything she ever wanted. When she looked at others, she expected to see others valuing her and desiring her company. Joey, on the other hand, saw potential hurt and abuse in his relationships. Celeste and Joey had two opposite childhood experiences, yet both reported problems in primary relationships.

If the only story you had read at this point was Joey's, you would be convinced that as a parent, you should try harder to be more positive, taking time to notice and comment on your child's assets, strengths, and contributions. But Celeste's childhood was filled with attention and positive reinforcement. What's going on here?

It is the concept of *balance* that is being addressed. Joey had a preponderance of negative messages while Celeste's was heavily weighted with positive ones. The result was that Joey's self-esteem was severely deflated while Celeste's was grossly inflated.

In Joey's case, it's easy to understand how negative messages came to be internalized. In Celeste's case, it's not so easy because it doesn't seem wrong to encourage and praise a child. In both cases, odds are that facts were overlooked and not mentioned. Joey's parent's never complimented him—in spite of the fact that there were many positives about him. Similarly, Celeste's parents routinely overlooked the negative, lavishing words of praise for the slightest effort.

Our parents aren't the only source of negative memories and problems growing up. Other adults, children, and our peers also help shape our self-concepts. Sometimes, our problems result from poor choices we make. In Joey's case, his fear of intimacy caused him not to initiate friendships. As a result, he was very lonely and never really had real-life friendship experiences. Today, he regrets the choice of not initiating friendships. Even Celeste has regrets. Because she was so valued by others, there were a lot of things she didn't try, because she did not want to risk failure or have to deal with others' disappointment. Today, when Celeste looks back at her life, she wonders what experiences she missed in her pursuit of others' approval.

Childhood injustices

Healthy discipline and honest feedback are necessary components of parental love and nurturing. When children suffer from neglect or abuse, they rarely afford themselves the luxury of connecting with the true self. Instead, with safety and love as overriding core needs, they assess others for how to react and how to be. Deferring to others in this manner is a form of abandonment, i.e., self abandonment. This is a coping mechanism that, once learned, is often rigidly held throughout adulthood.

If you are a victim of childhood neglect or abuse, consider carefully your adult decisions and coping styles. Are you re-victimizing yourself by not allowing expression of your true nature? In other words, do you speak your truth in relationships? Or do you hold back, fearing that you may hurt someone's feelings or, worse, that the other person might see all of your defects? Incidents of abuse and neglect in your childhood create the risk of becoming a victim again, or of becoming the abuser. *You are a victim in a relationship* when you are being harmed physically or psychologically and you feel hopeless to change it, believing that you are trapped. *You are your own victim* when you put yourself down or do things that you know you don't need to do. You are neglecting your needs if you are not asserting them or making a plan to address them or make them known. You are neglecting yourself if you ignore your internal longings and impressions. You are the potential abuser in relationships when you ignore others' needs, when you use them for your own personal gain, or when you cause physical and emotional harm.

Powerlessness, hopelessness, and unworthiness are just some of the feelings experienced by adult survivors of childhood injustices. If you experience these feelings regularly without understanding the source, you are likely being seduced by your childhood wounds. The true self is not powerless, hopeless, or worthless. The true self holds the keys to power, potential, and purpose. Sorting through these feelings and determining their source is important in moving through and beyond them.

Victims of abuse or neglect are at high risk to feel shame. This happens when we believe we are so unworthy that we split from our true selves and create false selves. John Bradshaw describes this in the preface to his book, *Healing the Shame that Binds You*:

> *What I discovered was that shame as a healthy human emotion can be transformed into shame as a state of being. As a state of being, shame takes over one's whole identity. To have shame as an*

identity is to believe that one's being is flawed, that one is defective as a human being. Once shame is transformed into an identity, it becomes toxic and dehumanizing.(vii)

Over the years, I have met a large number of clients whose true selves were shackled by shame. I know of no force that can terrorize self-expression as effectively as shame. I know of no more powerful way to disarm and mangle the self than to take on shame as an identity. Shame supports and feeds on self-doubt and self-criticism. The self that is immersed in shame has much difficulty being certain of the reality of an experience or the correctness of decisions. Shame causes so much second guessing of the self that even when a decision is made, the self manages to find a way to negate it by continuing to question it. Contentment is a state rarely experienced by the shamed person. However, as powerful as shame can be, it is no match for the present-moment awareness and forgiveness strategies found in later chapters of this book.

Becoming whole

While the childhood circumstances of many of us have tragic and life-long repercussions, the good news is that there is hope for healing. With each deferral of our true selves as children, we became more and more fragmented. Those discarded pieces and parts of our true selves lie in wait to be recovered, reclaimed, and granted space within our present lives. Challenging those childhood-inspired faulty beliefs, poor coping styles, and detrimental relationship strategies creates space for those discarded aspects to reenter our lives as part of a conscious choice to become whole.

In her book, *Breaking Free from the Victim Trap* (1989), Diane Zimberoff offers a glimpse of life after the healing of victim patterns and childhood wounds:

Once the victim patterns are released, the doors are open for you to truly become who you are. You will know on a very deep level what you feel, what you want, and exactly how to manifest it in your life. You will no longer be seeking approval from outside yourself. You will have the quiet confidence to experience the profound, authentic approval from within. You will be reunited with the spontaneous child within you as well as with the wise adult who makes clear decisions and wise choices. There will also be a loving nurturing parent inside that provides inner confidence. (p. 129)

Childhood and how the true self gets lost

Our childhoods are with us in more ways than we can imagine. In this chapter, we've looked at how negative experiences can result in negative beliefs about ourselves. Unchallenged, those beliefs become a functional part of a poor *self-concept*. In situations and relationships that matter, our *coping styles* often mimic those we observed in childhood. Similarly, our *relationships* often become a carbon copy (or an extreme opposite) of our childhood observations. The true self is not present when we are merely repeating learned strategies. The true self is present when we make conscious decisions about how we think of ourselves, how we cope, and how we interact with others.

This chapter has detailed a few of the ways in which our childhood experiences can keep us from connecting with our true selves. Your experience is uniquely yours. The following exercise may be helpful in stimulating your thinking with regard to your experience.

Exercise: Consider the following questions:

1. How did the parenting you experienced affect who you are today? Were you over-indulged? Neglected? Abused?
2. Describe your parents' positive and negative personality traits. Are you similar?
3. Your parents modeled relationships for you. What do you think is an ideal relationship? What were the spoken or unspoken rules of relationships that you observed growing up?

4. How did your parents handle differences of opinion? How do you handle them?

5. What are your coping styles? Which are functional (helpful to you) and which are not?

6. Do you suffer from shame? If so, what personality traits have you developed as a result of that shame?

7. Do you abandon yourself? How? If you do abandon yourself, make a plan to reverse one of these self-destructive behaviors.

8. Do you victimize yourself or others? How? If you do victimize yourself, make a plan to reverse one of these self-destructive behaviors.

Culture is not just an ornament; it is the expression of a nation's character, and at the same time it is a powerful instrument to mould character. The end of culture is right living.

—William Somerset Maugham
(1874-1965)

Chapter Two - Culture and the Self

We exist within the invisible framework of numerous cultures. We live within the culture of our country, our state, and our community. We interact regularly within religious, family, and business cultures. And each of these entities separately and together has formal and informal rules about how to be and act. Oftentimes, the culture even dictates how we should think. Is it any wonder that without questioning the spoken and unspoken rules of those cultures, the true self can get distracted and misdirected as it moves through life?

Nathaniel Branden, author of *Six Pillars of Self Esteem* (1994), uses the term *heroic exception* to describe those who preserve their self expression, self-esteem, and integrity within their cultures. He says:

> *In any culture, subculture, or family in which belief is valued above thought, and self-surrender is valued above self-expression, and conformity is valued above integrity, those who preserve their self-esteem are likely to be heroic exceptions.*(p. 292)

Celeste and culture

Consider the culture in which Celeste was raised. She lived in a small community in the rural south, in the heart of the Bible belt. Celeste, along with her parents, actively participated in their church. Her social activities as she grew coincided with the church's activities. Celeste attended Sunday School and Worship service nearly every Sunday from birth to the age of twenty-one. If Celeste missed one Sunday, she could expect phone calls from church members checking on her. She went from children's Sunday school classes to the youth group, and eventually the young adult group. Celeste had a beautiful voice and sang in the choir. She made cakes and washed cars for missions. She helped with vacation bible school. Celeste was a big part of her church family.

Over the years, the church members observed with tight lips as Celeste went through an enormous number of boyfriends. When

Celeste announced her engagement, the whole church seemed to breathe a sigh of relief that Celeste was finally going to settle down. Church members hosted numerous wedding showers and events in her honor. The wedding was well attended. Celeste was a beautiful bride with an equally handsome husband. Everyone left the ceremony believing that this couple would, without doubt, live happily ever after.

Imagine the surprise of church members when Celeste and her new husband started missing church. Within a month of the marriage, rumors of arguments and bruises were rampant. Celeste stopped singing in the choir. The pastor dropped by the couple's home to offer assistance but was told everything was fine. Church members called to check on Celeste but got no further than the pastor. Celeste and her new husband's names were added to the church's prayer line. Within three months of the wedding ceremony, word came to the membership that Celeste had filed for a divorce. With renewed effort, concerned church leadership and members contacted Celeste, only to be greeted by emotionless eyes and a false smile.

Within three months, Celeste's status in the church had fallen from model member to troubled, endangered member. Her parents were inundated with calls of concern for their daughter. Celeste had broken the unspoken rule of this church culture in that she was not working with the system her church had put into place to prevent divorce. Celeste knew she was not doing what was expected of her but just couldn't bear talking with others about her mistakes. She silently watched as members offered advice on how to save her marriage. She listened indifferently when told that she had not given the church a chance to help her marriage.

Celeste knew how the church felt about divorce. In her eyes, she had let down her church members. She no longer sang in the choir or participated in extracurricular activities. She attended church sporadically. Celeste had tied some of her sense of worth to the approval of her church community. When she looked into the eyes of those members, she saw her own disappointment in herself reflecting back to her. She endured the silent scrutiny without comment, sinking deeper into self-doubt and dislike.

Celeste felt lost without the admiring eyes of others. This same community had supported, praised and valued her for her entire life. She was still the same Celeste. Couldn't they see that? She could barely drag herself to services on Sunday. Those admiring glances had changed to looks of pity, disapproval, and disbelief. Celeste had let down everyone who had ever mattered to her. She had not realized how much her own sense of worth had been supported by the community at large. Celeste spiraled downward emotionally. She felt helpless to change her church community's view of her. Her parents and grandparents were also disappointed in her. If she could share with them what had happened, they might understand. But she could not. She could barely believe it herself. The only thing she knew for sure was that she had to follow through with the divorce—though the pressure to stay married was more than she ever imagined.

Looking back, Celeste knows she did the right thing. She knows too, that when she divorced, she lost her super-girl status in the church. The story of Celeste's marriage and divorce gives us a glimpse into one area of her life in which there were cultural expectations. Her divorce sparked multiple challenges on other fronts—with her family, friends, co-workers, and others.

Celeste's mistake resides in the power that she gave to her church and its culture to define her experience and to affect her self-concept. Celeste eventually grew to redefine this experience as a self-preserving measure, a matter of personal safety and integrity. Using language inspired by Dr. Branden's quote, Celeste's decision to divorce was a serious step toward preserving her self-esteem and becoming the *heroic exception.*

Please note that another person in similar circumstances attending the same church may have viewed the offers of support from church members differently than Celeste did. Instead, they may have seen those offers as gestures of love, which validated their self-worth. The point is that each person's experience is individual. To adequately understand the impact of your church on your self-development, you are encouraged to examine your own unique experience.

Cultural rules

Culture plays a significant role in identity development. In a different environment, Celeste might have been able to resolve her need to divorce her husband without self-condemnation. Culture restrictions can be helpful or hurtful. With the goal of rooting out the negative impact of harmful culture restrictions, let's consider additional examples of the spoken and unspoken rules in our lives.

- Church culture rules
- Family culture rules
- Other culture rules

Church culture rules

Daily religion class was a big part of my Catholic upbringing. I don't consciously recall a lot of what I learned, but I know that I learned a moral way of life. I learned the Commandments of God and the Laws of the Church. From an early age, these laws shaped how I viewed myself, as well as others. If I followed the laws (the rules), my self-concept was good. If not, I was a bad person. I also applied the same rules to others and judged them accordingly. I was taught that the Catholic Church was the only true church and that those who were not Catholic would not be able to go to heaven. Interestingly, I was told the opposite by non-Catholic kids I met growing up that I would not get to heaven if I was Catholic.

As I got older, I realized that there were all kinds of conflicting ideas regarding how to live within the religious communities of my town. Some churches allowed dancing. Others didn't. Some churches frowned on the use of makeup or pants for females while others didn't comment on those issues at all. I heard of churches that kicked people out while others welcomed anyone with open arms. What was right? Which rules were correct?

For an extended period in those school-age years, we were required to go to confession weekly. This resulted in a pattern of searching within myself for things I did wrong. Although it did not seem like it back then, my weekly confession was probably pretty mild. I'm sure it contained a list similar to, *I yelled at my sister. I did not do as my parents told me. I was mean to my brother.* But what developed in me was an unhealthy tendency to search only for the wrongness in me. My fears grew with my certainty that God was mad at me. Looking back, it seems that a simple strategy of looking within for what I did *right*, in addition to what I did *wrong*, may have offset the sense of faultiness with some semblance of self esteem.

I remember one day when I was thumbing through the Bible, I ran across this phrase: "The Lord will come with fire. He will ride on the wings of a storm to punish those he is angry with." (Isaiah, 66:15). That phrase really scared me. I lived in a place where thunderstorms were pretty common. So, without exception, *for years*, when storms were on the horizon, I examined my conscience for what I'd done wrong. I recall looking up at the sky on many occasions filled with fear that the Lord might have seen me disobey my parents.

Looking back, my church-related experiences revolved around rules: *I should be good. I am good if I follow the rules. I am bad if I do not.* Somehow, even though today I think I did a pretty good job at being good back then, I spent a great deal of my childhood with a deep seated belief that I was a bad and defective person.

My childhood self-concept suffered because I concluded that I was bad or faulty. *But this does not mean that all Catholic children grew up believing they were bad. This was my experience. Someone else might have internalized the same experiences in the same church differently and flourished from it.*

My task today is to make sure that none of those past negative and faulty beliefs affect my self-concept, my present moment relationships, or my coping styles.

Consider your own situation. There are questions in the exercises at the end of this chapter that will assist you in looking backwards. Odds are, though, if your church or religious upbringing affected you negatively, you probably know it. The task is to determine whether that experience is still in your life.

Keep in mind that low self-esteem, shame, and guilt thrive in rule-driven systems. A cautious religious leader of a church can empower the church members by separating the act from the person. In other words, the *action can be viewed as sinful*—yet the *person can be affirmed as divinely created and capable* of proper action. In addition, teaching self-forgiveness and compassion can diminish the negative impact of a perceived sin. (These strategies are discussed in Part III.)

Family culture rules

Our families are a huge source of rules, both spoken and unspoken. The list of potential rules that children are exposed to is vast and varied. Similar to church related rules, formal and informal rules put in place by families and peers can work for the benefit of children and families. Children thrive in an environment with healthy structure and discipline. Rules are necessary. Positive rules within families teach and enforce values and good moral character. Sometimes, however, rules can be taken too far. The result is a restrictive environment, where the child's individuality is not allowed to flourish.

Joey's environment was highly restrictive. There seemed to be a different set of rules for him than for his brothers. Here are just a few of the self-imposed rules that Joey bought into in order to survive emotionally within his family:

- I should never defend myself to a family member. (It will always be my fault anyway.)
- I should not look people in the eye. (They will get angry.)
- I should not speak. (I will be ridiculed.)
- I should try to stay away from my family members. (They will hurt me.)

Whenever Joey broke any of the above unspoken rules, he risked an argument or physical altercation. His true self was severely restricted.

If Joey had belonged to a support system of friends, he might've been able to compare their family rules and behaviors to his. In doing so, he might have been able to see that his family was not the norm. But, unfortunately for Joey, he had few friends. His restrictive environment stalled his self-development.

Some rules are often passed down through generations without question. Here's an example:

Grandmother never wanted to hurt Grandfather's feelings. She was worried he would get mad at her. As a result, she repressed her true self by holding back things she wanted to say and not addressing issues that needed addressing. Meanwhile, mother (as a child) watched silently from the sidelines, observing relationship rules about not hurting someone's feelings. When mother has children and her child wanted to share a negative opinion about a friend with her, she said "If you can't say anything nice about people, don't say anything at all." And the rule was in place.

Sometimes, a family does not have enough rules. I have worked with a number of young children and adolescents who were allowed to do what they wanted, when they wanted. Based on my experiences, this was neglect, i.e., neglect of a child's basic needs to feel safe, protected, and loved.

I'll never forget the remark made years ago by a young client of mine. He came to his first session with bruises on his arms and legs from the beating his mother had given him for not doing what he was told. Obviously holding back tears, this young man said to me, "I just wish my mom would tell me no and mean it!" He had never really had rules. Both his parents worked long hours. He was a latch-key child and was accustomed to doing what he wanted, when he wanted. As he got older, he expected more and more independence. Power struggles occurred when his mother decided she did not like the crowd he was hanging out with. Think about that comment again. "I just wish my mom would say no and mean it." I remember looking at him in disbelief and asking him to repeat what he had just said. Sure enough, same sentence. I am sure I asked him what it would take for him to know that his mother meant it. I don't recall the answer, but that is probably because he responded with an age-appropriate shoulder shrug. There definitely was a strong, rebellious nature in this young man, but there was also a little boy in him that longed to be nurtured and protected. Kids need boundaries. They need a fence within which to roam. Think of that fence of rules as loving, protective arms.

The rules that we are, or were, exposed to create our *shoulds*. Both Celeste and Joey were great at *shoulding* when we first met. Joey thought he *should've* tried harder to listen to his wife. Celeste thought she *should* never have gotten married. Spending too much time *shoulding* ourselves is debilitating to the true self. Did those *should* statements serve Celeste or Joey in a positive way? Absolutely not. The use of *should* resulted in more depression and anxiety for both of them. Within therapy, we abolished the use of the word from their vocabulary. With that word gone, there was space for more healing, affirming words.

Using the word *should* in our self-talk sets us up for depression. If you tell other people what they should or should not do, you risk coming across as judgmental and controlling. If I had my way, we'd ban that word from the English language. Many, many of my clients show up for counseling with an arsenal of *shoulds*. I hear, "I should've called her." "I should act right." "I should've known." "She should've written to me." "He should've told me about that."

No doubt about it. We grew up with rules, lots of them. Some served us well, others didn't. In our search for the impact of the rules we live by and the judgments that accompany them, we can listen for how we use the word *should*.

Other culture rules

Within our culture we are bombarded with advertising aimed at changing our tastes and creating new wants—wants that often go above and beyond the needs or wants of the true self. We tend to take that information and create guidelines (and rules to live by) for ourselves. We're cool if we have the latest shoes or the hottest cell phone. More importantly, we're not cool if we don't.

And what messages do we get about our bodies? The media often portrays tall, thin, and near anorexic women as beautiful and desirable by equally good looking men. Many, many women compare their bodies to those billboard and magazine bodies. In the process, many decide their bodies are not worthy. Unfortunately, some will choose to dishonor their basic physical needs to obtain that body, and that is a serious compromise of the self. On the other hand, consciously deciding to reject the current *thin as a stick* cultural norm (in favor of a healthy body) can be a self-supportive step in the right direction.

In our search for our true selves, we can ask ourselves if we are allowing the media to unduly influence our choices. For example, if we drive a car (or buy a purse, a pair of shoes, a boat, etc.), that we cannot afford we are compromising our self due to a faulty belief or action of some sort.

You may also find lots of unspoken rules where you work. I recall one day during a period when I was employed at a bank, a co-worker made a comment to me about my shoes. She said: "You're not supposed to wear white shoes after Labor Day." I suppose that was a cultural guideline I had missed growing up. At one of my first jobs, I remember that everyone stopped working at exactly 10:00 am for a fifteen minute break. No matter how busy we were, the break was a priority.

But think about more serious rules. What if the unspoken rule is that nobody goes home until all the work is done? What if doing all the work requires an average of 70 hours per week? And I only signed on for a 40-hour-a-week job? Do I change jobs? Or do I speak up to personnel insisting that I work the hours that I was hired to work? Am I a bad person because I want to work reasonable hours?

The point is that defining ourselves based solely on cultural expectations can move us dangerously away from our true selves. Likewise, blindly following cultural expectations can restrict our individuality. To maintain integrity with ourselves, it is important to develop an aspect of ourselves that is willing to go within and consciously choose to accept or reject the cultural expectations.

These are just a couple of examples of cultures that we live within. Our own experiences and day-to-day activities and interactions take us in and out of various cultures.

Cultural biases

Once we belong to a culture, we tend to use it as a base for comparison; in other words, we tend to believe that our ways are the only right ways. When we look at the beliefs of another culture with an eye for its inferiority, we judge the culture and limit our understanding. Whether it is our church, our political party, or our country, we tread on unsteady ground when we believe that our way is the only right way. Culture has a way of defining comfort zones that may or may not be good for humanity as a whole. It establishes within us internal battles, as well as battles of us vs. them, right vs. wrong, etc.

In Celeste's case, growing up, she accepted the cultural norms of her environment. For years, she believed her way of life was the right way of life. Her life circumstances caused her to examine those rules and decide to go against them. To survive emotionally, Celeste had no choice but to question the beliefs and subsequent rules of her culture.

If we can accept that our culture might be biased in certain ways, this will make space for the examination of our own values and beliefs.

Being the *heroic exception*

We are the *heroic exception* when we listen for the voices of our true selves and act accordingly. This does not mean that we bulldoze over others' needs to have our way, it means that we don't allow ourselves to be restricted. It means that, at the very least, we express our thoughts on what's happening in our culture, whether it's the culture of family, community or country. This type of expression allows for all points of view to be heard, for diversity to be honored, and for judgment to be diminished. Ultimately, it can foster change and new cultural standards due to honest and open discussion based on the beliefs and ideas of the members within that culture.

Culture, and how the true self gets lost

In summary, our culture can interfere with our connections with our true selves by providing rules for behavior that are not consistent with the inborn rules of the true self. A culture can provide a standard of measurement that we may not want, or be able to, live up to. This can drastically affect our *self-concepts.* If we can't live up to our culture's rules, we are at risk of judging ourselves as faulty or defective. This often keeps us from following the parts of our true selves that long for growth and change.

Coping styles are also affected by cultural dictates. If we have a poor self-concept, our coping choices may be to remain silent. We may tend to ignore problems rather than put ourselves on the line. If our coping styles are to do what everyone else does, this definitely does not leave room for developing individuality. With a poor self-concept and inadequate coping skills, we risk lowering our standards in *relationships.* Both factors affect interactions with others.

This chapter contains a few examples of ways in which living within various cultures can keep us from connecting with our true selves. Your experience is uniquely yours. The following exercise may be helpful in stimulating your thinking with regard to your experiences.

Exercise: Consider the following questions.

1. What are the various cultures/subcultures within which you live?
2. For each culture identified, what are its spoken and unspoken beliefs, values, and behaviors?
3. Are you comfortable with those cultural tenets? If not, in what ways do they inhibit the expression of your true self?
4. What are your *shoulds*? Did you create those *shoulds*? Did your culture create them for you?

5.   What would your life be like without any *shoulds*? What would your relationships be like?

6.   How is the culture(s) you grew up in still affecting your identity today?

7.   Has your culture affected your choices with regard to your career, relationship, spirituality, health, or wealth?

8.   How can a person be an individual within a culture?

9.   What cultural rules have you purposely broken because they did not fit you? How did you feel afterwards? Are you glad you broke those rules?

You don't have to listen to any voice that does not bring you peace.

—Author Unknown

Chapter Three - That Voice in Our Head

There is a presence in my psyche. Its voice tone ranges from provocative to angry. Its intention is never good. Its goal is to wreak havoc in my inner life and to prevent personal growth. I don't know how it got there. I'm not talking about psychosis. I'm talking about a form of self talk that I refuse to claim as coming from my true self. After all, how can I possibly lay claim to self-talk like, "That was a stupid thing to say," or "You look ridiculous," or "You can't do anything right."? If I listened to that voice, I wouldn't be sitting here typing text for this book, and I probably wouldn't have made it through college. In fact, if I let that voice control me, I'd be in a state of anxiety, or depression and self-doubt on a regular basis.

That presence that feeds me and you with all that negative talk has been given various names over time. It's been called the false self, the false ego, the sick self, the negative ego, and just plain negativity. I've even heard it called the voice of Satan. I prefer to call it the negative ego.

I'd like you to think about the messages of your negative ego and how those messages have affected you. As a counselor, I'm privy to hearing the negative ego's voice as it speaks through the mouths of my clients. I've listened as others have berated themselves and their efforts. I've witnessed the agony of limbo caused by the negative ego's paralyzing discourse. I've noted the hurt and anger that arises when the negative ego is in control. It's gotten easier and easier for me to recognize its tactics. I'd like to share with you what I have learned to keep you from falling prey to the negative ego. You can't avoid the negative ego. It's in your psyche too.

I can't say with certainty when or how the negative ego begins to exist within each of us. It's likely been with us our entire lives, from birth through childhood and into adulthood, where many of its arguments and strategies are woven into our daily lives. The negative ego has witnessed all the events of our lives and can be relied upon to give a negative spin at opportune moments.

In this final chapter on how the true self gets lost, I discuss the negative ego's role in keeping us disconnected from our true selves.

Emotional red flags

The negative ego's messages are often very compelling. Without due diligence it sounds (for a while) like our true selves talking to us. At other times, it sounds like a critical parent, speaking with authority, quick to notice everything wrong, and comment on it repeatedly. Once we allow its voice to reign free in our psyche, the negative ego can be relentless, bombarding us with self-blame and guilt-inducing thoughts.

Waves of negative emotion are sometimes the first sign that the negative ego has struck! Feelings of anger, unworthiness, defectiveness, defensiveness, shame, and guilt (among others) signal that a fearful negative ego is gaining hold of our emotions. And in the grips of these emotional states, it's difficult to do the work needed to access our true selves. Think of these deeply-felt, dark emotions as important clues to undermining the negative ego's influence in your life. If a thought provokes anxiety, fear, or depression, you might want to question the source. Think of the negative ego as controlling the lens through which we view the world. With that power, the negative ego has the means to skew our perceptions and play havoc with our present moment reality and our emotions.

Imagine the following self-talk going unchecked:

I really thought I was going to get that job. Now what? Why did I even think I could get that job? I knew better. I look like a fool for applying. I'm never going anywhere in this company. I'm never going anywhere, period. I'm a loser. How am I going to support myself and my family? I'm nearly broke. I give up.

Those thoughts would bring up negative emotions in most of us. Here's an example involving strong negative emotions:

Ed is driving down the highway, going to work. He starts to tailgate the car in front of him. When that car doesn't budge, he feels anger rising, his face gets red, and he's tempted to bump the car in front of him.

Ed's strong emotion of anger is the first clue that the negative ego has him in its grips. At first glance, he may not recognize that the negative ego is involved. When this is the case, he has probably encountered a similar situation so many times that he feels the emotion before he can catch the thoughts. In other words, the negative ego can work at lightening speed. After lots of repetitions, a whole string of thoughts can run through his mind in a nanosecond!

Using the above example, Ed's negative, ego-generated, judgmental thoughts may have been:

> *That guy doesn't need to be on the road.*
> *He needs to put down the (expletive deleted) phone and pay attention.*
> *He's going to cause a wreck.*
> *Idiot!*
> *What does he think he's doing?*
> *He's doing this to irritate me.*

As in this example, we can let the strong emotion serve as a red flag of the negative ego's presence. Once we can recognize its presence, we are more likely to be able to diffuse it. In later chapters, I will discuss specific strategies for dealing with strong emotions in the moment.

Negative ego themes

In addition to strong emotions, there's another way to recognize when the negative ego's messages are stirring up trouble. There are common themes behind those messages. Most of them involve the theme of separation, judgment, or comparison.

Separation is the primary theme used by the negative ego. Learning to recognize and watch for separation themes is helpful in discerning the source of the information (our true selves' intuition or the ego's voice).

The word *separation* implies *apart from* or *disconnected from* another person, place, or thing. When our thoughts create a distance between ourselves and others, or even from ourselves, it's likely that the negative ego is the culprit. Separation messages often involve seeing others or ourselves as superior or inferior, and thus the illusion of separation is present. Often, when the negative ego employs a separation strategy, we find ourselves judging others or ourselves negatively.

Consider Joey. His childhood experiences caused him to be extremely vulnerable to his negative ego's messages. Joey's belief in his defectiveness was fertile ground for the negative ego. But Joey wasn't a coward. He wanted to make friends and attempt relationships. He would go on outings to places where he knew he would find singles like himself. Once there, his negative ego would kick in, seize his psyche and, before he knew it, he was headed out the door. In the early days of counseling, Joey was unable to separate his inner voice from that of the negative ego. When the negative ego was in charge, here are some examples of the types of thoughts that emerged:

> *She won't look at me. What's her problem? She's so rude. She's only answering my question with one word answers. She doesn't like me. Why not?*
>
> *She won't look at me. I wonder if my shirt and tie don't match. I wonder if she thinks I'm ugly. Or maybe she thinks I'm overweight. What am I doing here?*
>
> *He won't talk to me. He must know I'm a fraud. I don't know what I am talking about half the time. I'm shaking inside so much, I'm sure everyone notices.*
>
> *She won't talk to me. Just like her friend. Someone must have told them something about me. I wonder who did that. I'm tired of people talking about me! I'm leaving.*

Can you hear the theme of separation in those thoughts? It was present in at least three ways:

- the decision not to get to know the person better
- the negative judgment of the other person
- the negative judgment that he was defective in some way.

Joey was *judgmental of others* when he saw them as rude and/or he perceived that others were talking about him. He was *judgmental of himself* when he launched into self-criticism. These thoughts brought up unchallenged fear and anxiety in Joey, which resulted in Joey leaving the scene. Joey's opportunities for true intimacy were severely limited with the negative ego reigning unchecked in his psyche.

The good news is that Joey, armed with awareness and purpose, did learn to challenge the negative ego. Here's the type of internal dialogue Joey learned and practiced to stop the separation and judgment:

> *She won't look at me. I'm beginning to feel rejected by her but I sense the negative ego's theme of separation behind that idea! So, for now, I'll just keep trying to talk with her. Those thoughts of rejection don't mean anything. Those thoughts are a negative ego tactic.*
>
> *He won't talk to me. I'm beginning to feel insecure. I know the negative ego supports that feeling. I'll just hold my head high and keep talking. I will NOT let the negative ego push me around like this.*
>
> *She won't look at me. I'm starting to get angry at her. What is that about? I've learned that the negative ego is behind the judgmental thoughts that I'm starting to have. I won't give those thoughts any credence.*

As Joey challenged the negative ego with more and more frequency, his progress in therapy and in life grew exponentially. He described himself as feeling lighter, like a huge burden had been lifted from him. And he actually did look lighter and freer. He looked people in the eye more often as he talked. He walked with more confidence. People noticed it, and they noticed him.

I wish I could report that the negative ego disappears into nothingness once we gain control over it. The truth is that it seems to hang out in the psyche waiting for a weak emotional moment to seize control again.

Comparison is another strategy employed by the negative ego to ensure separation. If we compare ourselves with others, we put our esteem on the line and we usually come up short. More importantly, when we compare ourselves to others, we flirt with being judgmental. The language of comparison causes conclusions driven by beliefs of *better than* or *less than*.

Celeste was very good at comparison. Whether she was at work, walking down a city sidewalk, or driving her car, she was scanning and observing. After all, Celeste had been groomed with beliefs of superiority. She watched others to notice who was noticing her. Her learned way of feeling good about herself was to note the verbal and non-verbal positive feedback from others.

Here are some examples of Celeste's inner dialogue in a work-meeting situation prior to making positive changes in her life:

Look at him. He's smiling at her in a way he's never smiled at me. What does he see in her that he doesn't see in me?

He's put a lot of time into his presentation. He used animation and sound files. I didn't have time for that. My presentation is going to look second rate next to his. I'm going to pretend to be sick, go home, and rework my presentation.

She really didn't dress appropriately for today. I am glad I wore my best suit. She looks awful in that color. Somebody needs to tell her that. I can wear that color but she sure can't.

The negative ego's theme of comparison was behind Celeste's thoughts. She compared the way someone reacted to another female to the way they reacted to her. She compared her presentation to that of another employee. She compared her attire and appearance to that of another female employee. In all three cases, someone came up short. Celeste's perceptions were driven by thoughts of being less than or better than the other person. Here are the kinds of thoughts that Celeste had to develop before she was able to show real progress in therapy.

Look at him. He's smiling at her in a way he's never smiled at me. That's interesting. How he looks at her has nothing to do with me! I will NOT compare. I will NOT empower my negative ego.

Look at his presentation. He put a lot of time into it. What a great idea to add sound and animation! My negative ego wants me to compare but I refuse! My presentation stands alone. I've always done a great job.

She really didn't dress appropriately for today. Where did that thought come from? Nope. Not going there. That's just my perception. I allow other people to be who they are. I don't need to use them as a false means of bolstering my self-esteem.

As Celeste learned to challenge the tendency to compare, she minimized the negative ego's influence in her life. The end result was that she began to settle in to the task of identity development. With the comparison strategy diminished, she was able to look within to make decisions about herself.

If we find ourselves always coming out on the positive or negative end of comparisons, we may eventually develop strong feelings of loneliness and isolation. This occurs because others (consciously or unconsciously) sense our assessment and, at some level, pick up on our belief of *better than* or *less than*. With either belief, we are inviting conflict or submission in our relationships. In such a case, intimacy never develops fully.

Taking it a step further; if we compare ourselves to others, we are demonstrating a value driven by *a desire to be the same as or different from someone else.* Given that forward progress on our life's journey requires discovering and valuing the true self (as we are) we can imagine how much comparison can slow us down. The negative ego strategy of comparison limits the future by allowing others to dictate it. In other words, when we look to others for assessment of ourselves, we are, in essence, at the mercy of their level of functioning.

Confronting the negative ego and diminishing its effects can help us be more fully present in our interactions with others as well as with our selves. In a sense, when we are successful in identifying and discarding the negative ego messages, we become the observer of our thoughts, and we take responsibility for them. To be in the moment requires courage. When we empower ourselves to be fully present in this way, we disempower the negative ego.

Childhood and the negative ego

Odds are that the negative ego gained the most ground in our psyche while we were children. Early in childhood (preadolescence) we did not have the ability to adequately challenge negative statements made to us by ourselves or by others. If our parents or other important people were not there to help us filter through the negative self-talk that can arise with difficult or challenging situations, the negative ego was allowed free reign within our psyches.

The Negative Ego and how the true self gets lost

In summary, the true self gets lost when the negative ego goes unchecked. When this happens, we find ourselves putting ourselves down and having lots of self-doubt. This has a significant effect on our *self-concept*, resulting in low confidence and low motivation to try new things. Our true selves hear many degrading insults with no defense unless we are aware that those statements don't come from the true self.

With low confidence, our *coping styles* are at risk to be severely limited. When we have problems and need to cope, we have to deal with the negative ego's take on things, making it increasingly difficult to adequately cope. If we are stressed, the negative ego will add to the stress. If we have a problem, the negative ego will add some more to the list. Our coping style may be to just give up, to feel hopeless and overwhelmed. Or the style may be to just do what someone else tells us. In the meantime, the true self sits silently waiting to be accessed and empowered. Without adequate coping styles, we have difficulty working through problems and gaining the confidence that could naturally follow a success.

Concerning our *relationships* and relationship strategies, there are multiple scenarios that could emerge. These are just a few. Our lack of belief in ourselves might cause us to lower our standards in our relationships. We may find ourselves driven to win an argument at all costs, or we might simply give in to avoid the conflict. Or we may end up camouflaging all this dysfunction and present a very functional self to the world, but in this scenario, the self is driven by a need to cover up dysfunction.

So, how does negative ego help the true self get lost and stay lost? It distorts our self-image, generates fear and negative emotions. It utilizes poor coping mechanisms. All of this blocks or slows each of us on our life's path.

This chapter contains a few ideas about how the negative ego can prevent us from ever connecting with our true selves. Your experience is uniquely yours. The following exercise may be helpful in stimulating your thinking with regard to your experience.

Exercise: Consider your responses to the following questions.

1. How has the negative ego influenced your self-concept?
2. How has the negative ego shaped your coping styles?
3. How has the negative ego influenced your close relationships?
4. How has the negative ego influenced your work/school relationships?
5. Identify the theme or strategy that the negative ego uses most often with you. Is it separation? Comparison? Judgment?
6. Think of a situation in which you have felt strong emotion. Was the negative ego present in that situation? If so, how? If not, what are the thoughts that drove those emotions? Furthermore, did you judge the emotion or just recognize it and let it go?
7. If you've been able to identify some of the negative ego statements, take the time to develop some affirming phrases or sentences to offset them. Write them. Remember them when you need them.

Part Two – How to Recognize the True Self

There is a wealth of information that's available to us that can assist us in negotiating life experiences without undue influence from our childhood wounds, our culture, and even our negative ego.

In Part Two, we examine three primary sources of that information. First, we call on Jungian concepts to complete a personalized *shadow* assessment. With an awareness of our own shadow traits and risks in hand, we learn to recognize when our own issues cloud our perceptions in the present moment. A plan to balance shadow traits is presented. Secondly, we examine how dreams and other unconscious manifestations can provide personal insight and direction. Finally, we are encouraged to tune in to the messages of our physical body and to recognize how disease states often connect directly to our psychological state of health.

The goal of Part Two is the expansion of awareness with regard to the vast amount of information available to us for self-discovery and empowerment.

To honor and accept one's shadow is a profound spiritual discipline. It is whole-making and thus holy and the most important experience of a lifetime. (p. x)

—*Owning your Own Shadow* (1991),
Robert Johnson.

Chapter Four - Shadow and Shadow Work

Our shadow generally lies outside of our conscious awareness, making it difficult to recognize without deliberate work. We all have shadow aspects. Recognizing and acknowledging this is the first step of shadow work. Doing the work to identify and balance shadow risk areas is the second step. The final step is to do the shadow maintenance work by remaining vigilant to the concept of balance.

The highlight of this chapter is an exercise that helps identify our personal shadow traits and tendencies. With that information, we can begin taking specific steps back in time to reclaim discarded aspects of our true selves. Similarly, we can use that information to keep us fully present in our daily interactions with others.

Recognizing and acknowledging shadow

The elements of our respective shadows are very specific for each of us. While there may be broad cultural similarities, a look at one's personal shadow is the place to begin. As we move through life, we make choices about ourselves, including who we want to be and how we want to relate to the world. We choose personal qualities that we identify with, like kindness and acceptance, for example. Unfortunately, we cannot choose anything without rejecting its opposite. The result of all the choices we make is that, in doing so, we generate a list of *qualities* of how we will not be as well as *actions* we will not take. Those rejected aspects make up our shadow. For example, I like to think of myself as *compassionate and responsible*. In choosing those two traits, I have likely rejected being *unfeeling and irresponsible*. These rejected traits now make up a part of my shadow. This is a problem for me. This choice creates risk for me to overcompensate in choosing the opposite. In other words, in rejecting *unfeeling* and *irresponsible*, I am at risk of becoming too compassionate and too responsible.

Let me explain further. Imagine a see-saw with the traits and actions we have *rejected* on one end of the see-saw. On the other end of the seesaw, we find an extreme opposite of those traits or actions. Both ends compose aspects of our true selves. To deny either end is to deny half of who we are. Balance is needed. This is done by standing in the center of the seesaw, consciously aware of both ends. This balancing act can be precarious at times, but the time and effort spent on balancing are sure-footed steps toward discovering and empowering the true self.

Here's an example involving Joey:

Joey's co-workers would probably describe him as passive. This manifested itself in many areas of his life. At work, he wouldn't ask for a well-deserved raise. Whenever he was in a relationship, he wouldn't say what was on his mind. With any issue involving potential conflict or disagreement, Joey nursed his anger quietly. Joey didn't understand why it took an enormous effort for him to be assertive. To make matters worse, when Joey did get the courage to speak up, he came off sounding aggressive. As he became more aware of his shadow traits and tendencies, he realized that his decision to be passive had a source in his childhood. His shadow seesaw held *passivity* at one end while *aggression* sat at the other. Shadow work for Joey involved learning healthy assertiveness.

I ask every adult client who comes to me for counseling to complete a shadow assessment. The information that we discover together is woven into treatment plans. The knowledge obtained from the assessment is invaluable and usually points to the core issues that support the stated purpose for seeking counseling. None of us wants to have blind spots with regard to our personality or character. Shadow work increases awareness to the point that we can enjoy greater integrity and inner peace while operating within the present moment.

Shadow components begin to gather at very early ages. Some seem relatively harmless, while others can immobilize us. Before we begin to look at your shadow, I'd like to describe the source of some common shadow traits that I have observed while working with people.

- Many adults who endured a divorce as children swear they will never divorce. The shadow aspects involve never divorcing at one end of the seesaw with divorcing prematurely at the other end. The shadow work involves the objective consideration of the pros and cons of divorce as it relates to the situation.

- Many adults who were sexually abused as children have shadow seesaws that contain overprotecting their children. In a sense, these adults are projecting their own abuse onto their children. With overprotection on one end of the seesaw, neglect is on the other. The child's physical needs are overprotected while the emotional, social, and developmental needs are being neglected. Fears and dependencies can develop. Also, the parent passes fears and shadow content to the child. In other words, the child may grow up with few limits for his or her children, creating risk for abuse. The shadow work involves finding a healthy level of protection and allowing the children to take normal risks.

- Avoiding conflict is another common shadow trait that I encounter in those who come for counseling. The client can usually verbalize that, as a child, he or she observed heated arguments with hurtful words. The shadow aspects involve avoiding conflict on one end of the seesaw and being confrontational at the opposite. Balance is achieved when the adult develops the courage to speak up as needed in relationships in a firm, but kind manner.

As mentioned several times in the discussion above, children often become a reaction to or a carrier of their parent's shadow. Without realizing, a family may have a learned a way to cope that is passed down to each generation, creating a generational see-saw effect. Great-Grandmother may have been too strict with her children. Grandma responds by being too easy. Mama responds by being too strict. Daughter determines she will be easier on her kids. And the beat goes on. It is as if the shadow asserts itself across generations until conscious work is done to correct it.

One way that this dynamic shows up in families is when one parent is particularly harsh on one, and only one, of the children.

One child is singled out to be corrected and criticized, while the other children often engage in the same behaviors but aren't corrected for it. Often, in cases like this, the parent is projecting all of his childhood's negative traits or shadow traits onto this one child. What a burden for the child! Furthermore, it really shows. When I see families with this dynamic, the parent has a more harsh tone and facial expression with the shadowed child yet surprisingly, doesn't realize it!

I didn't get to meet Joey's parents, but if I could, I'm certain that he was the childhood recipient of his mother and/or father's shadow aspects. When Joey began working on balancing his shadow traits, he effectively began the slow and sometimes painful process of peeling away the shadow his parents had cast on him.

Identifying and balancing your shadow risk

Here are step-by-step instructions that I use with my clients and myself to begin to identify some of the more obvious shadow traits. As you compose your list of traits or actions, keep in mind that not everyone is stuck on one end of the see-saw for every trait identified. The exercises are designed to help you identify your risk areas. Having the risk in one aspect of your life, does not predict that you have succumbed to the risk. Your life experiences may have expanded your awareness to the point that you have sought balance in that area and eradicated the risk.

For ease of understanding, this exercise and explanation is divided into three sections:

- Finding your shadow seesaw
- Recognizing your shadow risks
- Doing the shadow work

Finding the shadow seesaw

Take out a piece of paper and a pen. An example of a shadow worksheet is used throughout this explanation to facilitate understanding:
1. List the names of five people who push your buttons, i.e., make you mad, irritate you, or get on your nerves. It may be that you

=2=2=2=2

like or love the person, but there are certain traits about them that irritate you. People tend to list spouses, parents, in-laws, children, siblings, friends, teachers, and even preachers. Think about people you work with, people you live with, as well as people in your past. Many of my clients feel guilty writing down a name. This is for you. You can tear up the names when you finish.

Who pushes your buttons?				
Names/ Events	Describe the behaviors or traits	List the *extreme opposite*	Hurt my relation- ships?	Hurt my true self?
Sid				
Pat				

2. Next to those names, list 2-3 adjectives that describe *the aspect of the person* that irritates you. Examples of common descriptions are rude, critical, disloyal, insensitive, etc. You can also describe *an action* that irritates you. For example: "He always tells me what I need to do." Or, "She never can make a decision."

Who pushes your buttons?				
Names/ Events	Describe the behaviors or traits	List the *extreme opposite*	Hurt my relation- ships?	Hurt my true self?
Sid	*Irresponsible*			
Pat	*Unfeeling*			

3. The next step is to find the extreme opposite of each description that you identified. To assist with the understanding of shadow's influence, place the word *too* (or an equivalent) in front of both descriptions.

Who pushes your buttons?				
Names/ Events	Describe the behaviors or traits	List the *extreme opposite*	Hurt my relation- ships?	Hurt my true self?
Sid	Irresponsible	too responsible		
Pat	Unfeeling	too compassionate		

4. In addition to people, events in our lives may have affected us in ways that create shadow. To complete your shadow assessment, think of the two worst things that have happnened to you. Emotional damage created by such events can leave behind a trail of shadow aspects. For example, if you have suffered through a bankruptcy, your shadow traits could include being too frugal on one end of a seesaw or continuing to spend on the other end. List these two events in the name column. Think about the extremes that could be associated with the event. List those in the traits column. Continue to the next section.

Who pushes your buttons?				
Names/ Events	Describe the behaviors or traits	List the *extreme opposite*	Hurt my relation- ships?	Hurt my true self?
Sid	Irresponsible	too responsible		
Pat	Unfeeling	too compassion-ate		
Bankruptcy	too frugal	spending too much		

Recognizing shadow risks

Now that you have identified your shadow seesaws, let's look at your risk. Keep in mind as you work with the opposites that you are at risk to be both. For example, after a long stretch of being too nice, a person may find some aggression leaking out unexpectedly and at inappropriate times.

1. Use a highlighter or place an asterisk next to the aspects that you identify with the traits most like yours. Most of the time, you will find that you do tend to be on one side of the chart more than the other. Sometimes you might tend to vacillate between one side and the other, depending upon the situation or person you are with. And, finally, you might also decide you are balanced in this area. If, you believe you are balanced, go through the steps anyway. This will assure that you stay balanced.

Who pushes your buttons?				
Names/ Events	Describe the behaviors or traits	List the *extreme opposite*	Hurt my relation-ships?	Hurt my true self?
Sid	*Irresponsible*	*too responsible*		
Pat	*Unfeeling*	*too compassion-ate*		
Bankruptcy	*too frugal*	*spending too much*		

2. For each highlighted word or phrase, ask yourself these two questions:

   • How is being (insert highlighted word) hurtful to my relationships?
   • How is being (insert highlighted word) hurtful to me (my spirit, my psyche, my *self*)?

Who pushes your buttons?				
Names/ Events	Describe the behaviors or traits	List the extreme opposite	Hurt my relation- ships?	Hurt my true self?
Sid	Irresponsible	too responsible	Resent others Keep others from learning	Ignore my needs, become depressed or angry
Pat	Unfeeling	too compassion- ate	Overlook faults or help too much	Ignore my needs while helping others
Bankruptcy	too frugal	spending too much	Conflicts over money due to im- balance	Ignore my monetary needs or others' due to fear

For clarity, please review these examples:

- How might being too _____ hurt my relationships?

Using the example of *too responsible*, it is *hurtful to my relationships* because I end up doing most of the work. Over time, I could grow to resent my partner, seeing him as lazy. My respect for him could decrease as I grow more and more unhappy. I could also inadvertently deprive my partner of learning experiences. In my *work relationships,* being too responsible also results in me doing most of the work. As my co-workers take breaks and enjoy their coffee, they're very grateful that I'm getting the work done. I burn out, and become angry and resentful of my co-workers.

- How could being too _____ hurt me?

Once again, using the example of "too responsible", it is hurtful to me because the underlying message to myself might be: *I'm not willing to take care myself. I'm tired. I allow others to take advantage of me because I need their approval. I'm not worthy; therefore, I must work harder than others to prove my worth.* Without conscious effort to change, depression or anxiety can set in.

Doing the Shadow Work

After you have reviewed all the opposites and have thoroughly considered the problems associated with your shadow aspects, it is time to get to work on balancing.

1. Pick one and only one of the shadow seesaws that you would like to balance. Changing the dynamics of shadow is not easy work. If you try to change too many at once, you set yourself up for failure. When you first begin, try to choose something that's fairly easy to measure. For example, I would choose being over-responsible over having low self esteem.

2. Take a few minutes at the end of every day to do an exercise that will help change the imbalance. Review the day, thinking of the trait or action that you would like to change. Using the example of the seesaw with *overly responsible* on one end and *irresponsible* on the other, ask "How was I overly responsible today? How was I irresponsible?" If there is time, journal your answer and consider alternate behaviors. If you have no time for journaling, simply consider the answer to the question.

3. End your daily shadow work with a positive anchor.
   a. Close your eyes.
   b. Reflect on a time when you were balanced in your area of concern. If you can't recall a time, then imagine a future situation when you feel balanced in this area.
   c. Allow yourself to experience the positive feelings that go along with making self-supportive changes in your

life. Inhale the feeling of success, exhale doubt.

d. When you are filled with positive feelings, physically
    anchor this feeling of success. You can do this by making
    a fist or touching a thumb and forefinger together. If
    you do this regularly, you can use your anchor to boost
    your confidence throughout the day. In other words,
    to access feelings of success in balancing your shadow
    traits, you can use your anchor at any time. Use of the
    anchor can immediately bring back feelings of success.

This method works! After five to seven days of asking this
question, the issue of being too _____ will break into your
awareness in the middle of an interaction. Changes will occur as you
begin to consider alternate behaviors and do the work to balance
shadow. You may find that a third party is needed to help you break
out of the pattern. In other words, it may be very difficult to make
changes because you don't know how to verbalize something or what
steps to take. When this happens, a counselor or other objective
third party can assist in exploring healthy alternatives.

Shadow maintenance work

In his book, *Owning Your Own Shadow* (1991), Robert
Johnson states: "The tendency to see one's shadow as out there in
one's neighbor or in another race or culture is the most dangerous
aspect of the modern psyche."(p.27) He further states: "Unless we
do conscious work on it, the shadow is almost always projected;
that is, it is neatly laid on someone or something else so we do not
have to take responsibility for it." (p. 31)

None of us wants to lay our shadow neatly on anyone else.
When we do that, we end up reliving old hurts and removing
ourselves from the reality of the present moment. To maintain
balance, here are a few things we can do:

• Refer to our shadow risk list regularly
• Watch for new shadow aspects
• Manage our perceptions

Refer to the shadow risk list regularly

Shadow has a way of creeping back into our lives if we do not keep the risks within our awareness. I recommend that my clients delete the names and keep a list of their personal seesaws handy so that the risks can be reviewed regularly. This can be accomplished by rewriting those seesaws onto an index card that can be carried in a wallet or purse. This keeps them close at hand for those times that they want to refer to them.

Also, it can be helpful to repeat the complete exercise every couple of years to see if anything new has been added.

Watch for new shadow aspects

Tuning in to our over-reactions is an excellent way to watch for shadow aspects. As we go about our day, anytime something triggers us to react in a disproportionate manner, we can ask ourselves if a shadow trait is involved. If it is something new that we have not worked on before, we can put it on our list. Odds are that we won't be adding too many new things to our list, but, occasionally a new one will show up.

I realize that, at first, this may seem like a lot of information. Don't be discouraged. Following these instructions and working on only one seesaw at a time keeps it simple. If you are too ambitious and want to change it all, you'll start feeling overwhelmed. Be patient with yourself. Your shadow has been with you for many, many years. Balancing takes time and attention.

Manage perceptions

The seesaw traits identified can skew our perceptions. It's as if we're wearing sunglasses tinted by our shadow influences, potentially filtering the truth out of a situation. To correct this we can remove the sunglasses by taking responsibility for our shadow. By knowing our risk areas, we are less likely to call someone mean, selfish, prejudiced, etc. without at least wondering what those words say about our own traits. Simply knowing that our perceptions are skewed in our shadow areas can help us seek the truth.

Observing a shadow aspect in someone else, our self-talk could go like this:

"This person is being *aggressive.* That's on my shadow list. I realize that my perceptions may not be 100% accurate as they relate to aggression. Am I really seeing aggression or is it simply healthy assertion?"

The reality is that sometimes the aggression (or other shadow trait) that we see *is* aggression. Shadow work merely requires that we consider that our perceptions might be skewed. The knowledge of our shadow seesaws and the associated risks helps us sort through these items in the moment.

The golden shadow

This chapter on shadow would not be complete without considering our golden shadow. Just as we reject negative traits growing up, we are equally capable of rejecting our positives traits. Jung called these rejected positive traits the golden shadow. In other words, if we find ourselves admiring someone else for anything, odds are that those traits are within us—but we have yet to develop them.

Take a minute right now and think of someone you admire. What is the trait that you admire in that person? Accept that it is also in you. What keeps you from displaying that trait?

Of the golden shadow, Robert Johnson writes:

"Jung warned us that it would not be too difficult to get the skeleton out of the closet from a patient in analysis but it would be exceedingly difficult to get the gold out of their shadow. People are as frightened of their capacity for nobility as of their darkest sides. If you find the gold in someone he will resist it to the last ounce of his strength. This is why we indulge in hero-worship so often." (p. 45)

Dreams and shadow

Our conscious world is not the only place where shadow lurks. As the light of day fades, shadow slips into our dreams where it plays the starring role in our worst nightmares. The next chapter will shed more light on the shadow characters and themes in our dreams.

Shadow work, and how to recognize the true self

In summary, our life experiences result in our rejection of certain traits or actions. Once rejected, these traits or actions have the potential to follow us around (like a shadow) until we integrate them back into our lives. We tend to express these rejected shadow traits in extremes unless we actively work to balance them. When we express a shadow trait, our *coping strategies* are often affected because our perception of the situation at hand (or the person) is likely to be skewed. We tend to project our own shadow traits onto others with whom we interact creating risk for problems in *relationships.* Our *self-concept* is at risk to suffer because shadow-laden interactions tend to replay old unresolved issues from childhood—situations which likely resulted in damage to our self-concepts.

Shadow work can help us recognize and connect with our true selves. Completing the shadow exercise reveals many of our shadow tendencies. Choosing one shadow seesaw with which to work begins the work of balancing and integrating the shadow. The net result of all of that work is the removal of past negative influences and the introduction of choices made by the true self in the present moment. In Chapter Eight you'll learn strategies for staying fully present in relationships.

The following exercise may be helpful in stimulating your thinking with regard to your experience.

Exercise: Consider your responses to the following questions.

1. What are your shadow traits? How do they play out in your thoughts, emotions, and actions? Imagine that you have balanced these shadow traits. How would your self-esteem, coping styles, and relationships change with that balance?
2. Take a look at your shadow traits. Have you had a past relationship with someone who has many, if not most, of those traits? Based on the information in this chapter, would a balanced approach with any of those traits have changed the nature of the relationship?
3. How have your shadow traits influenced your self-concept? Your coping styles? Your relationship strategies?
4. To which golden shadow traits are you drawn? Do those traits tie into any discarded career or life goals? Do you feel worthy to own and accept that you have these traits?

Dreams are impartial, spontaneous products of the unconscious psyche, outside the control of the will. They are pure nature; they show us the unvarnished, natural truth, and are therefore fitted, as nothing else is, to give us back an attitude that accords with our basic human nature when our consciousness has strayed too far from its foundations and run into an impasse.

—Jung, C.G. (1933). *The Meaning of Psychology for Modern Man.* In Collected Works, Volume 10: *Civilization in Transition.* p. 317.

Chapter Five - Dreams and Other Unconscious Manifestations

"Dreams give information about the secrets of the inner life and reveal to the dreamer hidden factors of his personality. As long as these are undiscovered, they disturb his waking life and betray themselves only in the form of symptoms." (*Jung*, 1933, *p. 16)*

These hidden factors, parts of us that have been repressed or rejected, can be viewed as fragments of ourselves that have only one purpose—to re-unite with that which pushed it away. The Self longs to be whole.

Imagine putting together a 1000 piece puzzle only to discover that three or four pieces are missing. This is frustrating with a puzzle but totally unacceptable to the self. With missing aspects, the Self is more vulnerable in the walk through life. With missing aspects, *we* are more vulnerable, i.e., more vulnerable to making decisions and choices that may not be aligned with our true selves.

The good news is that dreams do provide us with clues about those missing pieces. Much as our bodies produce extra white blood cells to assist in keeping our bodies functioning properly, the true Self moves toward healing (wholeness) by using dreams to present images, urges, and memories from the unconscious. Paying attention to those clues will help us locate those missing parts.

Here's a dream I had shortly after I made a decision to write this book:

I am walking with thousands of people down a crowded sidewalk. Everyone is wearing business suits and walking in the same direction. I veer off to the right and find myself on a pathway with only a few others. The path is wide and goes through the woods. I'm not afraid, but relaxed and content. A teenage girl runs up to me and gives me a hug and a kiss.

My initial thoughts about this dream were that it was about my profession (clue: business suits). The dream seemed to be saying that my current profession was not necessarily my only path. A different path presents itself. A teenage aspect of me was excited to see me on this path.

I knew that I had made the decision to write the book and saw the dream as encouragement from my inner self to do it. I was intrigued by the teenager who showed up to greet me. I thought about writing as a teenager and immediately made the association. In fact, in the summer between my junior and senior years in high school, I enrolled in an introductory English course at the local university. I loved to read. I loved my English classes. I was excited about having a chance to take a college-level class. The first assignment was to write a paper on the topic of our choice. I couldn't wait to write it. As soon as I got home, I started writing. I wrote, wrote, and rewrote until I was sure I had written a masterpiece in philosophy, which I entitled "Why?" I proudly turned in my paper, knowing that it was really good. I was certain my writing would impress this college instructor. When I saw the teacher come into the class with our papers in hand, I noticed mine was on top. I noticed lots of red marks, which did not serve to dampen my enthusiasm. In fact, I was absolutely certain that those red marks were words of praise! My world fell apart when the professor held up my paper to the class with a big red "D" on it. The memory of that big red "D" is imprinted in my mind. The words she said are not so clear but they went something like this: "Somebody had the *nerve* to title their paper "Why?" My memory is blank after that, other than shrinking into my front row seat as she handed me my paper. The bottom line is that, as a teenager, I decided then and there, I could not and would not write. No more thoughts about majoring in Journalism or being an English teacher! And so, I fundamentally abandoned that aspect of myself—which had been very real up until that moment.

My dream, therefore, was showing me that, in my choice to write, I was reuniting with this aspect of me, which had gotten stalled or been fragmented at that age. In a sense, one of my missing puzzle pieces had been found. Although the road to this book has been strewn with delays and frustrations, I have never forgotten that I must write this book. I must rescue this aspect of myself who is waiting for me on that path in the woods!

Parables of the Soul

Dreams provide overnight entertainment with subject matter that ranges from love stories to epic adventures. The stories and adventures in dreams are like parables, *parables of the soul*, images and ideas presented in metaphor and fiction that offer us an opportunity to decipher our own personal meaning, i.e., to gain awareness of the missing aspects and to offer a glimpse of the changes we need to make in order to re-claim our lost parts.

Like a good movie with deep meaning, we can continue to think about a dream and derive helpful insight from it for years to come. A great difference between viewing a movie and having a dream is that the dream bears a personal message intended for us and us alone. Rather than a made-for-TV movie, it is a made-for-me movie. Its message is personalized; we often have first hand knowledge of the actors! The dream's underlying message, no matter how frightening or strong, contains a message with a motive of personal peace.

The author of our dream adventures

For purposes of this discussion, we will assume that the author of our dreams is the true self, i.e., the part of us that knows the truth and sees beyond the misperceptions and illusions created every day in waking life. At night, the true self sends us messages about changes that we need to make in our lives and/or our thoughts. After listening to my clients' dreams for years, it has become apparent that dreams are not presented unless the dreamer is ready to make those changes. In other words, until the dreamer can deal with the issue and has the inner resources to pull them off, the information will not be presented.

I usually encourage my clients to ask (at bedtime) for a dream about something they need to know. Several times over the years, individuals have come back to me saying that they did not dream anything after this, but instead, slept terribly, waking up on numerous occasions. After hearing this repeatedly, I added a new dimension to the question. I suggested asking for a dream about something they need to know *and are ready to hear.* This immediately changed the experience for those who had problems. It was as if those restless nights were due to material that the unconscious wanted to present, but that the conscious mind was not yet ready to hear.

Celeste was an incredible dreamer. In our efforts to break the many patterns in her life, we turned often to her dream world. Celeste's dreams were filled with gunshots, death, anger, searching, and chasing. I recall one dream she had involving a caged bird that needed to be free. The caged bird was Celeste's true self, longing for freedom. At another level, it could be a messenger whose message had been locked away. Celeste's dreams of gunshots and murder were reflective of the parts of Celeste that were being wounded as she lived her life repressing and ignoring the intuitive impulses being broadcast from within. Celeste's desire to please others resulted in lots of indecision, uncertainty, and low self-esteem. After all, others' needs became paramount in her insatiable thirst for positive feedback.

Approaching the dream

By now, I hope I've presented a convincing case that dreams are a very useful way to access information about how to make changes that result in more personal happiness and inner peace.

Here is a good way to get started with dream interpretation:

1. Make the decision to begin to work with dreams.
2. Feel the excitement of knowing that access to a treasure trove of information, previously unavailable, is about to open up.
3. Place writing materials next to the bed so that you can easily record your dreams upon awakening.
4. Ask the true self to give you a dream with a message of something that you need to know about yourself. (If you wish, you can add the condition of wanting only a dream that you are ready to hear.)
5. Tell yourself that you will remember the dream.

6. Relax into sleep with the excitement of knowing you will get a dream answer and you will remember the dream!

This method works. If you don't dream an answer the first night, keep asking the same question every night until a dream occurs. Sometimes I wonder if there is some inner-dream-desire-skeptic holding back on the dream saying something like, "Let's see if they really want to dream. They'll need to keep asking until I'm convinced they really want this dream." Continuing to ask without getting discouraged helps dreams occur.

Deciphering the meaning of a dream

Unraveling the meaning of a dream is not a perfect science. The same dream can often have multiple meanings and messages. Two fundamental ideas that support the most thought-provoking psychological and spiritual dream interpretations are:

- Every aspect of the dream is an aspect of you, your personality and/or your waking life (past and present). This includes all objects, settings, actions, and persons.
- The dream contents suggest the diagnosis of a condition (albeit psychological) as well as the prescription of a remedy. In other words, dreams spell out for you the problem the psyche wants to resolve while also suggesting a solution.

Everything and everyone in the dream is a part of us

Everything and everyone in your dream is an aspect of you, your personality and/or an aspect of your waking life (past and present). Think about it. That's a strong statement! This means that the brother, the mother, the boss, and even that lost child in the dream are aspects of you, seeking attention. Furthermore, the car, the house, and the gun are somehow related to a part of you.

Yes, the ***characters in your dream*** are aspects of you! When you already know the people in your dream, you can think about your personality traits or what they might represent to you. Unknown people represent unknown aspects of you that are emerging or playing a role in your life without your full awareness. For example, an unknown angry woman would be an aspect of you that is angry and that wants expression.

The ages of the dream characters are also important. If a dream character is someone I know, but in the dream, they are a different age than they are today, that fact is an important consideration. For example, if I dream of an old friend but see her as twenty years old, I might first attempt to recall what was happening in my life at the age of twenty. I would wonder if there were any traits that I ascribe to her that were being expressed in my life at twenty. Let's say that my friend is *helpful and supportive.* I might wonder if a helpful and supportive aspect of myself was somehow wounded or got stuck at that age. The point is that any inconsistencies related to age need special consideration in the interpretation.

If there are children in the dream, the ages of those children are clues to an age when an unhealthy coping or identity decision about self was made. (In later sections, there is a discussion about dreams related to post traumatic stress.)

The ***setting of a dream*** is vitally important to its meaning. For example, if, in the dream, you find yourself in the house in which you grew up, then the dream is relating to that time in your life and how growing up in that house is still in your life today. Settings like schools represent learning and sometimes point to certain ages in your past. Churches often represent spiritual growth. A beach can be about areas of your life where you are beached (stuck), or they can simply represent a relaxing setting.

Objects in dreams have general meaning as well as specific meaning. An object that has been a part of the dreamer's waking life would involve that aspect of his or her life. For example, a gun in a dream that belonged to a relative would have different meaning than just any gun. Transport vehicles often show up in dreams (cars, trucks, eighteen wheelers, buses, trains, bicycles, etc.). These often represent issues regarding movement through life. If, for example, you are driving an eighteen wheeler, you might want to ask yourself if you are hauling lots of others' "emotional issues" around with you. A bicycle, on the other hand, can illustrate the personal effort you are making on your path.

The overall *feeling* of a dream is also important. Whether the emotion is fear, paralysis, excitement, or detachment, it adds the feeling element to the overall meaning. The presence of a strong emotion suggests questions like:

- What aspect of me is angry in my waking life?
- Are there areas of my life where I feel paralyzed or unable to make progress?

Often the dreamer is simply the observer and is detached from the emotion and the action. This simply suggests that the dreamer is being asked to observe the message of the dream. It might also be suggesting that the dreamer needs to detach from the issue presented to get a clear picture.

Reviewing the *actions of a dream* can also contribute to the meaning. For example, I recall an image from one of my client's dreams where he was in a car that was hovering upside down and spinning out of control at a four way stop intersection. The actions of this single dream image suggested the following questions:

- Was there any area of his life that felt stalled?
- Did he feel that he was at a crossroads in his relationships, career, personal growth or other aspect of his life?
- Did he feel out of control?
- Did he feel that his world turned upside down lately?

The specific actions in a dream often directly correlate with actions we take in our waking life. In my dream when I left the sidewalk to take a path in the woods, the dream reflected the waking choice to take a different career path. The action of a dream can also represent a suggested action (or prescription) for the dreamer to take in the future. See the next section for more information about prescriptions.

Looking for the diagnosis and prescription

I once had the privilege of hearing Robert Johnson, noted Jungian analyst and author of numerous books, speak about dreams. He asserted that dreams can diagnose a condition (describe our problem or situation) and prescribe a remedy (suggest a solution). In other words, the diagnosis aspect of the dream paints a picture of the issue to be addressed within the dream. The prescription usually involves a suggested action to take. Sometimes, the suggested action is implied. For example, when a client tells me about disturbing dreams that awaken him or her, I often think that the suggested action is to wake up to (become aware of) that issue in his or her life.

In the dream about choosing the path to write, the diagnosis goes something like this: In my current life, I am dedicating my time and energy to walking a path in my professional life that is not risky. There is nothing wrong with the path. Many have chosen it. There is, however, another path available—a path that could connect me with a teenaged aspect of myself. The prescription is to take the path less traveled.

Finding our personal dream meaning

Dream interpretation can be as difficult or as easy as we want it to be. The more time we have for it, the more specific meaning we derive from it. Here are some steps to get started:

1. Record the dream.
2. Give it a title.
3. List the setting, feeling, characters, actions and important objects.
4. Next to each item, list the personal meaning it has for you. If it's unfamiliar, think of the role the object has in the dream. Allow yourself to make associations freely. Write your associations next to the item. Look up a meaning in a dream dictionary, if necessary.

5. Consider all of this dream information and rewrite the dream with ideas about interpretation. Detail any insight into any specific area the dream addresses.

Let's apply this technique to one of Celeste's dreams. She had the following dream during a particularly dark period of self-doubt, indecision, and hopelessness:

> *I fell out of a canoe into a river that was flowing. The canoe had other people in it and kept going downstream. The only person I remember was my daddy. The river was full of snakes. I was trying to stay away from the snakes and stay afloat. I kept screaming for my daddy. I couldn't climb out of the water because both sides were made up of walls of rock that went straight up. I swam to the right side, turned around and swam to the left side. I just kept swimming back and forth, screaming, trying to stay away from the snakes. They were so big. I woke up scared and exhausted.*

Here's a list of the key elements in Celeste's dreams:

Title:	Trapped, Surrounded by Snakes!
Setting:	Flowing river between two insurmountable walls of rock
Characters:	Me
	Daddy
	Snakes
Objects:	Canoe
	Rock walls
Actions:	Falling out of the canoe
	Swimming back and forth
	Screaming for daddy
Feeling:	Fear
Diagnosis:	At some point in my life as I was traveling along, I stumbled and fell. This resulted in me being surrounded by fears. I am helpless and hopeless.
Prescription:	Get in touch with my daddy, my *inner father*.

Celeste's initial interpretation:

> *The fall from the canoe in the dream indicates my fall from the path or journey of my true self. My fears (the snakes) are keeping me from moving forward. I am exerting a tremendous amount of energy running from my fears. In a sense, I am trapped. I must let go of (or ignore) my fears, allow myself to go with the flow (go downstream) and I will reconnect with my inner father. A healthy inner father is the part of me that can be strong, supportive, and decisive. Developing a healthy inner father can keep me safe. I must move through these fears to keep moving forward in life.*

Word play in dreams

Themes and ideas in dreams are woven together masterfully. I recall a client whose dreaming self used the word *patients* in the dream to direct the attention of the dreamer to their expression of *patience*. With another client, the symbol of the *sun* was used to refer to her *son*. In another of Celeste's dreams there was a tiny, almost unreachable *bug* on her back. Her dreaming self was playing with the meaning of the word *bug*. That *bug* represented something that was *bugging* her.

Recurring dream themes

Over time, dream patterns and themes emerge for many of us. The same dream might occur for three nights in a row or once or twice a year for twenty years. If we have recurring dreams, odds are that our true selves are simply repeating themselves again and again until we get the point and start making changes. Our dreams with recurring themes will stop when we've heard the message and have taken steps to make whatever change is implied. Otherwise, we can expect to continue having the dream, often with increasing intensity.

For Celeste, her recurring dream theme involved wounded or hurting characters that needed rescuing. As time went by, the characters became increasingly immobilized. Consider this dream of Celeste's:

> *I was in a house with several high school friends. I was working on homework. All of a sudden, I started freaking out. I knew one of my friends was going to do something crazy. I heard her running bathwater. I ran in the hall. She was in the bathroom with the door locked. I screamed for her. I found another way in. My friend was naked in the bathtub. I didn't see any blood but I knew she had slit her wrist and was in cold water. She had passed out. She was unresponsive. With help from another friend I got her out of the bathtub, wrapped a towel around her and sat on the floor, holding her, crying, begging her to get better. I knew she wasn't going to die but my heart was broken because it had come to that point.*

Celeste had this dream at a time when she could not make the changes she knew she needed to make. This dream ***diagnosis*** suggested that she wasn't simply trapped, but that there was also a part of her that was suicidal, on the verge of giving up. Celeste was aware of the issues but kept making the same mistakes. Note in the above dream, Celeste had been studying (looking within for insight). While studying, she became aware of this aspect of herself that needed rescuing. The dream ***prescription*** was to get in touch with this wounded part of herself and to hold her, comfort her, and keep her alive.

There are other, more subtle dream patterns. A person might dream often of a specific setting or person. In such cases, special consideration needs to be given to the pattern. A recurring dream in a specific house from the dreamer's past might refer to a matter involving time spent in that house or with its occupants.

Nightmares

If our true selves have not gotten our attention in the waking world, we might find our shoulders being tapped vigorously in our dreams. This is no different than, say, a passenger in our car pointing out a red light ahead while we continue toward it without slowing. Eventually our passenger may shout for us to STOP. Using this analogy, the nightmare is the *friend*. Our true selves have tried to get through to us on an important matter of the psyche that we have neglected. The consequence of ignoring those clues is an emotionally charged encounter with ourselves, one in which we feel frightened, overwhelmed and/or attacked. And, to be certain, if we still don't get it, i.e., we still don't make necessary changes in our waking lives, the nightmare will recur again, often with increased levels of fear.

Think of nightmares as 911 calls from the true self! Using the information available from the content of the nightmare, we can examine and re-examine our waking world for problems that could knock us seriously off course. The dangers are almost always psychological, yet the death or serious wounding of the true self is as serious as, or more serious than, a physical wounding. Ignoring a nightmare is akin to speeding down a winding road covered with ice; we continue to move through our lives ignoring danger signals until an accident happens.

Recall from the shadow chapter, that the content of shadow is made up of aspects of ourselves that we have rejected. In nightmares, the rejected part can show up as a shadow part. For example, if our shadow harbors *aggression*, the monster in the dream that we fear could be the *aggression*. It's pursuing us so that balance can be achieved. The more we run from *aggression*, the larger it looms. In such a case, our dreaming self is reflecting our fear of *aggression*. *Passivity* sits opposite of *aggression* on the shadow seesaw. To move toward center from *passivity*, we'll need to discover *healthy assertion*. The bottom line is that if we are having a nightmare, we should consult our shadow list. One of those rejected traits may be trying to raise our awareness to some critically necessary change in our waking world.

Here's a portion of a nightmare of Celeste's that followed in the days after the snake dream. Celeste was screaming for *daddy* in that dream while she was swimming to avoid snakes. In this one, a dream *daddy* figure reappears:

...the oldest little girl was in the back seat floorboard of the car. Suddenly, I was her. I was reaching up for the mean daddy's hand...and he took a gun...and with the end of it... hit her (me) hard in the mouth and said, "You're not mine, you bastard child." I felt it in my mouth. I knew all my teeth were gone and blood was going everywhere.

In this dream, Celeste determined that the daddy figure represented an unhealthy inner father figure. The appearance of this figure suggested the significant levels of self-abuse and self-rejection in Celeste's waking life. Note that the first dream involved separation from the father figure. In this dream, a new and more threatening element is introduced. Both dreams suggest the need for the development of a healthy inner father figure. The increased intensity of this dream suggests urgent action.

In terms of shadow, *self-abuse* and *self-rejection* are at one end of a shadow seesaw with *too much self nurturing* and *too much self-acceptance* on the other. For Celeste, these shadow traits appear to be a result of the overindulgence she experienced as a child. Yet, as shadow traits tend to do, they haunted her present moment until she balanced them.

A side note: Nightmares can also be the result of a traumatic event or repressed memory. When you suspect either of these elements, or when nightmares continue to the point that they disturb your waking life, it's best to consult with a mental health professional for guidance and assistance.

Uncertainty about interpretations

If we cannot fully understand a dream or a particular symbol in that dream, we can ask for more information the next night, or any night thereafter. With persistence we will get an answer. The dream that answers our question may not initially seem related to the original dream. Regardless, we can trust that our dream request is being answered, and we can attempt to interpret the dream. When I've suggested to my clients that they ask for a dream to shed light on a previous night's dream, they often come back saying: "I had a dream but it didn't relate." I assure them that it probably did and we usually find a connection. If not, there are several possible explanations. First, the dreamer may not be ready to receive the information. Second, the dreamer may not really want to hear more information. In this scenario, the unconscious picks up and acts upon the underlying truth. Finally, the dreamer may already have all the information he needs.

Here are additional techniques for eliciting more meaning from a dream:

1. Create an imaginary dialogue with a character or object. Imagine the character or object in an opposite chair. Ask the person or object why it appeared in your dream. Allow answers to emerge. Trust what comes up. Continue the dialogue until you're satisfied that you've received the answers or that there aren't any more answers.
2. Act out the dream. Walk through it physically. Be each character.
3. Imagine sharing the dream with an audience, beginning with "Once upon a time, there was a dreamer who dreamt that…" At the end, tell the audience the "moral of the story."
4. Set aside the dream. Allow a few days for the meaning to emerge. With that intention, ideas can present themselves throughout the day. When this happens, it's helpful to take time to make a note. This shows our true selves that we are taking this seriously and fully intend to understand the dream.

A final word on dreams

There are numerous books on dreams as well as dream dictionaries available. Robert Johnson's book, *Inner Work* (1986), presents a thorough discussion on understanding and interpreting dreams. *Cloud Nine, a Dreamer's Dictionary* by Sandra Thomson is also an excellent reference. There are also dream definition websites. The one I consult the most is www.dreammoods.com.

Jung warns against using means outside of ourselves to determine the meaning of dream symbols. In *Man and His Symbols* (1964), Jung writes:

> *And, speaking more generally, it is plain foolishness to believe in ready-made systematic guides to dream interpretation, as if one could simply buy a reference book and look up a particular symbol. No dream symbol can be separate from the individual who dreamed it. (Page 38)*

Jung's statement got my attention, but I learned that, for me and many others, a dream dictionary can be very helpful in suggesting and broadening meanings. When I first started working with my own dreams, I used Sandra Thomson's guide with each dream. Today, I check it only occasionally to make sure I'm not ignoring a meaning. The point is, if we use a dream dictionary, we should also use our intuition. If a definition doesn't feel right, discard it. We can consult with a friend or family member if we're uncertain of a personal meaning. Ultimately, we are the only ones who can truly understand the messages in our dreams.

The purpose of this chapter was to introduce you to the idea of listening to your dreams for direction on your path to connect with your true self. I've presented some basic ideas to help you begin to understand of the messages in your dreams. *Please note that you do not have to follow every step of the recommended approach.* You can spend as little or as much time as you want with your dreams, but do spend time with them. Dreams are an incredible ally and resource on the road to self-discovery and empowerment.

Dreams, and how to recognize the true self

Dreams put us in touch with parts of ourselves that need expression or consideration. Dream themes and the messages they contain often relate to our present-day expression of *self-esteem, coping styles, and relationships*. Ultimately, working with the messages of dreams helps us in the development of self-awareness and insight.

The following exercise may be helpful in stimulating your thinking with regard to your experience.

Exercise: Consider your responses to the following questions.

1. Pick a dream you've had in the past. It can be a dream from childhood or a more recent dream. Apply the method described earlier to interpret your dream.
2. Do you have any recurring dream themes? Settings? People? Consider the significance of the recurrence.
3. Do your dreams reflect any shadow influences?

Our bodies contain our histories—every chapter, line and verse of every event and relationship in our lives. As our lives unfold, our biological health becomes a living, breathing biographical statement that conveys our strengths, weaknesses, hopes and fears.

—Carolyn Myss, *Anatomy of the Spirit*
(1996), p. 40

Chapter Six - Tuning in to the Messages of the Body

All of us recognize when our body tells us it's hungry, thirsty, or sick. We accept these basic communications from our body without question. Yet, our bodies communicate with us at many different levels. One way to tune in to the messages of the body is to recognize that it reflects our personal issues back to us. The key is learning to listen for its signals.

Do all illnesses have a personal message behind them? Maybe. Maybe not. The point is that often there is a message, so why not find it early and avoid unnecessary pain? Certainly, we inherit many of our *physical* vulnerabilities, BUT if we have poor *emotional* health, we can exaggerate and increase that vulnerability. Taking the time to consider possible connections between your physical and emotional health pays off in the long run with an overall improved physical condition.

Grace's story, debilitating headaches

Grace, fifty, had been on sick leave for three months when she walked into my office for the first time. She suffered from blinding, debilitating headaches that could last for hours. She had been to numerous doctors and endured countless tests to resolve the headaches, but no easily identifiable problem could be found. She had been prescribed everything from anti-inflammatory medicine to anti-depressants. Nothing seemed to help. When her last doctor suggested counseling, Grace decided she had nothing to lose and everything to gain by trying.

As Grace related her story, her compassionate and caring nature became evident. She seemed to easily (and eagerly) pick up on others' needs, sometimes before the other person even knew they had any! As she continued to talk, it became increasingly clear that in her relationships, Grace felt nearly compelled to meet others' needs, while at the same time, rarely considered her own.

In the twenty years that Grace had worked in the health care industry, others had often looked to her for support. Grace felt gratified to be able to help others. Over the course of time, others expected Grace to go the extra mile, i.e., to work late helping others while never asking for help herself. The end result was that Grace's expectations of herself grew far beyond her capability to fulfill her now inflated need to nurture others.

But work wasn't the only place that Grace's nurturing nature got her into trouble. At home, her desire to be a "good" wife and mother led to the eventual exploitation of her kindness. Grace's family looked to her for support and as time passed, became resentful and angry if she did not put their needs first or see their point of view. Grace's marriage was in jeopardy. Even her relationship with her children was strained and conflicted. Grace could feel her level of anger and frustration growing with her family and with herself. She felt trapped and saw no solution.

Think of a small child that wants to be heard. At first he calls your name. If you don't answer, he tugs at your jacket. If you keep ignoring him, he begins to shake the jacket vigorously. Finally, the child shouts or hits you to get your attention. This is what was happening with Grace. Her physical body, via her headaches, was hitting her hard to get her attention.

When clients report physical ailments to me, I take the approach that everything is perfect. In other words, Grace's headaches are perfect in that they are trying to get her back into a more balanced and healthy state of being. The headaches, then, are a means the body uses to communicate to Grace that change is needed. In trying to understand the message of Grace's headaches, I asked: How are these headaches "helping" Grace? What is the symbolism of the specific location or action of the illness? The answers were:

- The headaches resulted in Grace needing to rest. She was on leave from work.
- The headaches resulted in others offering to nurture her. And the headaches required that the other family members in Grace's household take care of their own needs.
- The head is in the physical area of the intellect, i.e., "knowing." There was pain in the area of "knowing."

Those ideas led to these questions for Grace:

- What is it that *wears you out* or causes you to feel *overwhelmed* or *exhausted*?
- Who nurtures you?
- How do you nurture yourself?
- In your family relationships, what is it that you *know* you must do but you don't do?
- At work, what is it that you *know* you must do, but you don't do?
- If you chose to nurture yourself more at work and at home, what changes would occur?
- Are you willing to assert your needs in your relationships?
- Are you willing to balance your nurturing nature by nurturing yourself?

Grace was ready for change. Her headaches dissipated quickly as she demonstrated to herself that she was willing to do whatever she needed to honor the messages of her body. She spent the next couple of months in counseling, discussing boundaries and learning how to communicate and assert her needs. At work, Grace volunteered less and began to delegate more. She raised her expectations of others at work and at home, and in so doing, gained their respect. In the end, she was grateful for the lesson provided by those headaches. You'll read more about Grace and her relationship challenges in Chapter 8.

Tuning in

In Grace's case, the headaches were very loud communications from her body. There was no way she could ignore them. Often, however, it is possible to be at such a heightened state of stress that you don't even notice that you have pain or discomfort anywhere in your body. I can attest to this based on a minor recurring health problem that began when I was an undergraduate student. The problem persisted until I graduated with my Master's degree. Every semester, without fail, I developed cold symptoms a few days after the end of the semester. (And this was right at the time when I would want relax and enjoy myself.) If it was a short break, the illness would usually last until the start of the next semester. It was as if I had been pouring all my energy into that research paper, those math problems, that history test, etc., without noticing that I was tired, sick, or pushing myself. I was in a heightened state of stress, *driven by perfectionism*, which commanded that I do well on every assignment. When the semester was over, I could finally relax. BUT, without fail, I would get sick.

What was happening? What was my body telling me? Looking back, it is easy to see that I was ignoring my body's signals for rest, etc. Instead of tuning in to my body's messages, I was fueled by my stress induced adrenaline. (By the way, I also ignored my own intuition, which suggested that I could stop striving and would do well anyway.) Relentlessly, I forged ahead making myself vulnerable to the most prominent virus of the time. I recall drinking caffeine loaded drinks to stay awake, taking 20 minute power naps at 3:00 in the morning, and doing whatever it took to meet deadlines. In the process, I ignored my body's messages and paid the price with a weakened immune system.

So, yes, I was in a heightened state of stress at the end of every semester. I didn't recognize symptoms as they were occurring. Instead, those symptoms hovered in the background and emerged full-blown when I could finally relax and let go of my stress. If I had been more in touch with my body, I would have heard its cues early and taken steps to prevent the illness that was brewing in the background.

In my case, the illnesses were relatively mild. In Grace's case, the illness was more serious and debilitating. In both cases, not listening for or hearing the messages of the body resulted in illnesses and missed work. Both could have been avoided.

Reducing the level of stress in our bodies helps us tune into our bodies' signals. To tune in, we can create a stress reduction routine. Using it daily helps calm us enough to connect with the physical experiences of our bodies.

If you don't have a daily routine, here's something you can try:

1. Find a quiet place in your home or in a peaceful nature setting. Plan ahead so that you won't be interrupted. Turn off your cell phone. Tell others of your intention to be alone. Put on quiet music, or just enjoy the natural sounds of silence.

2. Close your eyes and begin to focus on your breath.

3. Imagine that as you breathe, every molecule of your entire body, including every skin cell is engaged and inhaling with you. Inhale deeply. Draw the air into your abdomen. Fill the abdomen with your breath until it extends (like a balloon).

4. Exhale completely. Again, imagine that every molecule of your entire body is participating in the exhale.

5. Repeat. Imagine that each inhale brings a sense of peace and calm. Each exhale expels stress and other negative emotions.

6. Repeat until you begin to notice the shift from stressed to peaceful and calm.

7. As you continue to breathe, scan your body section by section, searching for any feelings of tightness or discomfort.

8. For each area in which you find tension or discomfort, focus the breathing on that area as you breathe. If the discomfort doesn't dissipate, start an internal dialogue with it. Ask the discomfort what its message is. Continue to breathe as you wait for a message in the form of a thought, symbol, or simply knowing. Whether or not you get a response, thank the uneasiness for its message and tell it that it can dissipate now as you will take its presence and message seriously.

9. Continue breathing slowly and steadily until you feel that your body is completely relaxed. Enjoy the relaxed state for as long as you like. Open your eyes.

In the above exercise, if you note an area of tightness, pain, or uneasiness, consider the location and any possible associated meaning.

Whatever area of the body feels constricted, consider its function, then work to establish meaning via metaphor and symbolism.

For your reference, see the chart on the last page of the chapter for possible general meanings of pain or discomfort in specific body areas. For more detailed meanings, there are several books written on understanding the messages of the body. The two that I use the most in counseling are: *You Can Heal Your Life* (1984) by Louise Hay and *Anatomy of the Spirit* (1996) by Carolyn Myss. Both books have excellent reference sections devoted to matching an illness to its corresponding psychological or spiritual counterpart.

Meditation

A regular meditation routine can assist in keeping our stress levels minimized so that we can tune in more easily to the shifts of energy and changes in our bodies. At the end of the above stress reduction exercise, an additional period of meditation is recommended in order to enhance your connection with your physical body.

There are numerous meditation techniques. One technique is to simply focus on the breath for an extended period. Another might involve listening to selected music. Still another could involve guided imagery. Information on meditation is readily available in retail stores and on the internet.

Illness language

My clients often inadvertently reveal their current or potential future illnesses to me. Someone who talks about others being a *pain in the neck* may find themselves with neck pain. Here are some other expressions with implications of physical consequences that I've heard many times:

It just wears me out!
It breaks my heart to think...
It's killing me to know...
It pains me to think about...
It scares me to death...

It strikes me…
I can't support myself…

We can expand our awareness to catch these words and phrases before we express them, and then change by replacing them with a more accurate description of what we are trying to say. For example, instead of saying, *it scares me to death*, we could say instead, *I am extremely frightened.*

About physical symptoms

Physical symptoms often accompany very real physical problems. We honor the needs of our bodies when we consult a physician to address biological causes of our pain and discomfort. The information in this chapter offers some secondary meanings that may be helpful in discovering the psychological message.

Tuning in to the messages of the body, and how to recognize the true self

The messages of our physical pain can put us in touch with repressed or unexpressed emotional pain. Those messages, once deciphered, arise with self-healing and self-connection as a goal. The source of these messages is our true selves. Our true selves long for healing and wholeness. We recognize and acknowledge our true selves when we tune into our bodies' messages and take the necessary steps to heal. Making changes based on those messages can result in improved *self-concept, coping styles, and relationships.*

Beginning with the next chapter, we look at specific strategies to address some of the problems that may reveal themselves within those body messages.

This chapter contains a few ideas about the ways in which tuning in to the messages of our bodies can give us clues on changes that can connect us with our true selves. Our experiences are unique. The following exercise and chart may be helpful in stimulating thinking with regard to our personal experience.

Exercise:

1. Do you have any past or current illness, aches, pains, or body discomfort? If so, what are some potential meanings?
2. Think about people you know who have illnesses. Can you associate anything about their illness with a psychological meaning? For example, someone with a heart problem may have suffered a broken heart in his or her close relationships.
3. Do you use any phrases that reflect any past or current illnesses?
4. Ask a close friend or family member to point out to you if/ when you use illness and death words while talking.
5. Develop a daily routine to tune in to your body. Note any tension, aches, or pain. Dialog as needed. After working through this routine for several days in a row, you may find that you can complete the whole process in five minutes. Spend as little or as much time as possible.
6. Review the chart on the next page for any past or present aches or illnesses. Are your shadow issues reflected in any of your illnesses?

(See table, next pages...)

Possible Meanings for Body Discomfort

Head
Face

The senses of hearing, seeing, tasting,
smelling and processing of thoughts are located in this area.
- What am I having difficulty facing?
- Do I see too much or not enough as I move through my day?
- Do I overlook important details or do I do the opposite, spending too much time focusing on details?
- Do I hear too much or not enough? n other words, do I read between the lines or not hear what is actually being said?
- Do I overanalyze or worry too much?
- Do I think things through in a healthy manner?
- What is it that I know I must do that I am not doing?

Throat
Neck

The functions of communication and swallowing
are located within this area.
- Do I speak my truth in my relationships?
- Do I hold back or not say things to keep from hurting others?
- Do I repress myself by not expressing my ideas and feelings?
- Am I too blunt and straightforward?
- Am I having a hard time swallowing something, i.e. some idea or belief?

Chest
Heart
Breasts

Functions involving the sustenance of life are
found within the chest area.

- Am I trustworthy and reliable?
- Do I trust others too much or not enough?
- Do I have any matters of the heart that are unresolved or need attention?
- Do I nurture others/myself too much or not enough?

Back

Two functions of the back involve carrying
weight and maintaining balance.
- Am I balanced in my support of others and myself
- Do I nurture others/myself too much or not enough?
- Am I overburdened?
- Do I have good boundaries?
- Do I take on too much responsibility?

Hands   The hands give, receive, create, express, assist and defend.
                 • Am I a giver? A taker?
                 • In what areas of my life do I feel powerless or have too
                   much power?
                 • Am I taking time to develop and express my creativity?
                 • Do I offer assistance, or am I too dependent on the
                   assistance of others?
                 • Do I stand up for myself? Do I stand up for others
                   when I feel called upon to do so?

Stomach   The stomach and the related digestive parts process, sort,
                 and derive nutrients while expelling waste.
                 • Do I adequately process and sort what I perceive to be
                   another person's negative opinions of me, or do I allow
                   them to carry too much weight?
                 • Do I give too much weight to my own perceived
                   mistakes and faults, resulting in low self-esteem?
                 • Do I hold on to things too long without dealing with
                   them?
                 • Do I have unresolved resentment and anger?
                 • Do I try to find the good in others as well as in myself?

Feet   These body parts have in common functions
Joints   related to movement and balance.
                 • In what areas of my life am I stuck, or moving too fast?
                 • Am I leaning (depending) on someone else too much
                   or vice versa?
                 • Do I need to reconsider a direction I'm taking?
                 • Am I too flexible? Too inflexible?

Please note that the above chart is intended to challenge with questions that address the state of psychological health. Consult your physician for diagnosis and treatment of physical ailments.

Part Three - How to Heal and Empower the True Self

Armed with the awareness from previous chapters that we are not always fully present in the moment, we learn in this section how to use that awareness to seize opportunities *in the moment* for healing and empowerment of the true self.

In Part Three, we review four common areas where opportunities for healing exist in our daily lives. We examine our emotions and explore techniques to defuse or set aside negative emotions. We explore relationships, triggers, and methods of defusing triggers. We learn to access and speak our truths. Finally, we embrace forgiveness as a strategy for healing our own wounds and maintaining integrity in the moment.

The short-term goal of this section is the introduction of strategies for deliberate present-moment living. The ultimate goal of this section is the healing and empowerment of our true selves.

There can be no transforming of darkness into light
and of apathy into movement without emotion.

—Carl Gustav Jung (1875-1961)

Chapter 7 - Using Emotions to Empower the Self

Emotions are a natural part of each of us. Happiness, excitement, joy, etc. are easily recognized emotions and positive expressions of our true selves. When we're in a genuinely positive emotional state, we can relax, knowing we are in sync with our true selves and our needs in that moment. Negative emotions like anger, hatred, resentment, etc. are also easily recognized, but because of their negative nature, are often rejected, repressed, or over-expressed. Most of us spend little, if any, time questioning or challenging those emotions and their purposes.

Strongly felt emotions, especially negative emotions, often signal some kind of disconnection from or attack upon the true self. By learning to recognize these emotions and to insert a reflective pause into them, we gain command over these emotions, creating opportunities for empowerment and healing.

Cognitive behavioral theorists suggest that emotions don't arise without provocation, although sometimes that may appear to be the case. Instead, these theorists suggest that our thoughts precede and lead to our feelings. In other words, other people, situations, or events cannot be legitimately held responsible for our feelings. Taking command of our thoughts empowers us to choose our emotions and emotional responses.

Recall from Chapter 3 that the negative ego often introduces themes into our thoughts. Putting to work the techniques in this chapter will also minimize the negative ego's influence over our day-to-day experiences.

Joey's thoughts

Recall that Joey had a pretty difficult childhood, growing up with neglect as well as physical and emotional abuse. His style of negative thinking began at a very young age. From his point of view, he never received validation from others. He learned to go within himself in difficult situations and look for someone to blame. These tendencies continued through adulthood. Here is an example of one of Joey's depression-inducing internal dialogs:

I think they're mad at me. I don't know what to do. Why is everybody always mad at me? I must be doing something wrong. What did I do to make them mad at me? Why does this keep happening to me? It's not fair. I'm always the one who gets blamed. I'm sick of this. Any time I try to be close to anybody they start being mean to me. I just can't get anything right. I give up. I'll never be happy.

Looking at Joey's train of thought, we can understand how his initial thought (a thought that occurred often in childhood) could lead to other thoughts that result in feelings of depression.

Celeste's thoughts

Remember Celeste? Pampered and praised her entire childhood, she expected the man in her life to give her his undivided attention. Her problems began when her current boyfriend would want time alone or a night out with his friends. Celeste's pattern included an initial anger response followed by desperation and hopelessness. The thoughts that fed these emotions went something like this:

He makes me so mad! He isn't telling the truth. What's he really going to do? He's a liar. Who is he really going to be with? Why doesn't he want to be with me? What's wrong with me? I'm fat. I'm ugly. Nobody wants to be with me. Nobody will ever want me. I'm so lonely. I'm going to end up an old maid. I better call him and apologize.

It's easy to see how Celeste's litany of self-demoralizing talk could result in feelings of despair and hopelessness. The more this pattern occurred in her life, the quicker she could go from "He makes me so mad!" to "I'm going to end up an old maid." I venture to say that just prior to counseling, Celeste could run through all of those statements and jump to feelings of despair in about half of a second.

Let's look at some alternative thought processes for Celeste and Joey. We worked within therapy toward changing their self-talk to go something like this:

Joey—*They seem mad. Hmm... I wonder what's going on with them. I'm fairly certain I've been above board and considerate in all my interactions with them. In the past, I used to think I did something wrong. I'm glad to be over all that self-blame! I'm so much more aware now. I'm getting better and better!*

Celeste—*He doesn't want to be with me. Interesting thought...am I just reading into his actions or has he actually said he does not want to be with me? I'll just pay attention. Right now, I feel some fear that I recognize all too well from my old pattern. I'm going to proceed slowly without being reactive and perceiving rejection. The facts, the flowers, the cards do not support rejection. Wow! What a difference it makes to be able to take charge of my thoughts! I'm doing great!*

Although the differences in the above sets of dialogs are very clear, there are significant and noteworthy similarities. In both cases, *the thoughts (self-talk) preceded the emotions and dictated the experience.* In the first examples, the thoughts led both Joey and Celeste to negative emotions (anger, depression, despair, hopelessness, etc.) In the second set of dialogs, the more positive reflections keep those feelings at bay, making space for hope and self-empowerment. Learning to witness and gain control of their thoughts allowed both of them to be in the present moment and actually opened the door for self-empowerment. The key point is that *the difference is the choice of thoughts.* The power to recognize and change self-talk is a significant strength that we can draw upon to carry us through life's many challenges.

Once we accept that emotions result from thoughts, we can learn to watch for those thoughts and challenge them. Actively working on self-talk involves recognizing a negative emotion and then backtracking to pinpoint exactly what we were thinking just prior to the appearance of these emotions. Once we identify the thoughts, we can begin to formulate more deliberate (and often more truthful) thoughts. In doing so, we learn to reverse the downward emotional spiral that can occur when we let our negative self-talk get out of control.

While Celeste and Joey needed counseling to make this significant change in their thought patterns, some of us already have built-in positive thinking styles. Our inner resources and strengths determine this ability to bounce back from these types of thoughts. Regardless, we can recognize when we're caught in a negative thought process if we allow our thoughts about a situation to take us into a negative emotion.

Learning to change the channel

Changing the channel is my personal favorite technique for changing my self-talk. Consider that self-talk that plays in our heads is like a radio broadcast. Using that analogy, imagine that we have multiple channels that we can access at any time, and, most importantly, that we can change the channel at will once we learn to exercise our power to do so. Without realizing, Joey and Celeste were spending a lot of time tuning into the negative thought channel. Joey and Celeste ultimately learned that they could change the channel to a more empowering channel, which might be called the *Self Empowerment Channel*.

We have the power to pull out of a negative emotional state by making a choice to change the channel of our inner radio broadcast. We are, after all, the only member of our listening audience. As the negative self-talk airs and emotions like anger or sadness begin to present themselves, we can exercise our options to change channels. We *do not* have to feel these feelings.

On any radio broadcast, if we don't like what's playing, we can hit the *scan* button or use our remote to find another more appealing station. Think of negative thoughts as being broadcast from the *Negative Thought Channel*. Once we recognize that we are listening to this station, we can immediately begin to scan for a more impelling, uplifting, and encouraging channel. Doing so significantly increases the odds of countering the energy of a negative thought assault.

Using the analogy of the radio broadcast, here are the steps for changing the channel:

1. **Decide to recognize when a negative broadcast has begun**. The decision to listen for our own litany of self-criticism is sometimes enough to create recognition. A visual reminder that we are trying to break this pattern can

be helpful. We can consider wearing a rubber band around our wrist, putting a post-it note on our mirror, or similar technique. If catching the words does not work, recognize that the presence of negative emotions can often signal that something or someone may be messing with our radio tuner. Negative feelings often manifest physically in the head (*head is spinning*), the neck (*constriction of the muscles around the neck*), the stomach (*queasy feeling*), or the chest (*a sense of tightening*). The physical experience of negative emotions varies widely among individuals. The presence of physical discomfort can alert us to the possibility that we may have tuned into the wrong broadcast.

2. **Once the recognition has occurred, pause**. *Pausing our thoughts* is equivalent to recognizing that we are listening to music we don't want to hear and directly checking the radio dial to see what station is playing. The more practice we get at pausing, the easier it becomes. In the examples with Joey and Celeste, the pauses are reflected in the words "Hmm…" and "Interesting…"

3. **Listen for the negative self-talk that supports the emotion**. Once we are able to pause, we have the power to reflect on the music (thoughts) that have been broadcasting unencumbered. This step draws on present-moment awareness. It is important to the empowerment process that we identify the words and phrases that require challenging.

4. **Change the channel by replacing the self-talk with more accurate and encouraging words.** If we've been able to accurately identify the negative self-talk, this step is relatively easy. For example, if you hear yourself saying, *"I'm a terrible parent,"* you can challenge that thought with, *"This isn't true. I work very hard to support and encourage my children. They know I'm here for them."* On the other hand, if you can't seem to find the specific offending thoughts, that's ok. Have a general empowering sentence or short paragraph memorized and ready to use. Use your

sentence (or sentences) until you can more accurately determine the specific thoughts. For example, you might try: *"I'm getting better and better at recognizing and stopping negative feelings. It feels good to be in control of my emotions."* Repeat your sentence over and over again until you begin to feel emotional improvement. I'll offer some additional strategies in the following section for situations in which you can't identify the offending thoughts.

The above steps take time to master. Each step leads to the next. By this I mean that we cannot complete step two until we have mastered step one. Likewise, step three won't work until we grasp steps one and two. With the first three steps in hand, we are ready for step four. And, when all is said and done, we have succeeded in giving less air-time to negative thoughts. We've also discovered that we have the power to command our present-moment emotional state.

Dealing with sudden onset

There are times when we experience negative emotions very quickly and strongly. It might appear that we've bypassed the words and gone straight to the emotion, but this is unlikely. More likely is that we have had the preceding self-dialog so many times that the response becomes automatic. A *conditioned response* has developed. In other words, when others push our buttons, we have a complete negative dialog in a fraction of a second, and we leap into a negative emotion or action. With these dynamics in place, it can be much more difficult to recognize and challenge the self-talk.

The following techniques can serve as temporary safety nets, until we regain our composure long enough to recognize that we do have the power to change the channel.

1. **"Cancel! Cancel!"**
   Use the words "Cancel," to counter invasive thoughts. This approach can be likened to trying to talk over music being

broadcast. It can and does work, but you must repeatedly address the thoughts you want to eradicate with that word. Once the volume of the thoughts (and accompanying feeling) have backed down somewhat, it will be easier to change the channel.

2. **"Chill Jill!"**

A similar technique is to give those crippling thoughts a name and tell them strongly to be quiet and stop talking! Prepare for using this technique by coming up with a short name (preferably of someone you don't know). Then, when you hear a thought like, *"nobody likes me,"* or *"I'm always messing up,"* shout aloud (or to yourself) *"Stop Jack!"* or even *"Chill, Jill."* This approach seems to work better when you choose a one syllable name. Be sure the name is not yours or the name of someone you know. If so, it could be distracting and dilute the process. Giving those thoughts a name can be very effective because, in a sense, you are externalizing the thoughts, recognizing that they (the thoughts) do not belong within the present moment.

3. **"I'll think about that tomorrow!"**

Try the Scarlet O'Hara approach. At the end of the 1939 movie classic, *Gone With the Wind*, Scarlet is standing outside her beloved home, Tara, with fire blazing in the background. With only remnants of her home left standing, she stubbornly states, *"I'll think about that tomorrow."* In doing so, Scarlet has *scheduled her worry*. If we find ourselves emotionally charged about an issue whose outcome is totally out of our control, we can announce to ourselves, *I'll think about that from 8:00 – 9:00 tomorrow.* When 8:00 tomorrow arrives, start worrying as much as you can until 9:00. If the issue comes up again, reschedule it. Repeat this process until you recognize that you do have control of your thoughts and, therefore, your emotions.

When thoughts and negative emotions go unchecked, many people develop emotional and physical symptoms. I have met many clients who were referred to me after showing up at the emergency room with symptoms like heart palpitations, profuse sweating, difficulty breathing, etc., only to discover that there was no physical cause for their symptoms. In those cases, the client's condition was considered a panic attack, a condition in which the thought-fed feelings spiraled out of control. Individuals who experience panic symptoms can improve their condition by changing the channel techniques. (Working with a counselor is likely to increase the odds of success.) Many negative symptoms respond positively to a deliberate, calming, self-talk strategy.

Triggered?

Thoughts are behind many episodes of negative emotion, but, it is also important to recognize that strong emotional reactions that are not logically related to the present moment may be caused by a trigger. Triggers can be thought of as aspects of our present moment that effectively link us (consciously or unconsciously) to a past unresolved issue. When triggered, we might find ourselves overwhelmed and immobilized by a seemingly innocuous issue. For example, if we find ourselves in the depths of despair because a friend can't go to the movies with us, the despair is unlikely to be related to our friend. Instead, it is highly likely that we've been triggered and are experiencing the feelings related to a rejection (or other issue) from years past. We certainly can benefit from attempting to change the channel when triggered. In addition, it's important to recognize that the strong emotion may have a story to tell. Specific strategies for dealing with triggers in relationships can be found in the next chapter. Strategies for reducing (and potentially dissolving and healing) the impact of triggers can be found in each of the remaining chapters.

Freedom of emotional choice

Within counseling, not too many days go by in which I haven't heard the following phrase: "*He/she made me feel…*" The phrase is usually attached to an emotion-word like *angry, sad, guilty, unhappy*, etc. Think of the absurdity of that kind of statement. How can anyone possibly *make* us feel a certain way? People don't hold a gun to our heads and say, "*Be sad or else.*" If we control our thoughts, and therefore, our feelings, no one can make us feel anything. We truly choose how we feel. We choose our response. Believing that others can make us feel a certain way empowers them, while making us the victim. We don't have to be at the mercy of someone else's thoughts, moods, or actions. We reclaim our power when we stop giving it away to others. If we hear ourselves using that phrase or something similar, we can rethink the situation. For example, rather than allowing ourselves the convenience of the thought *He made me angry*, we can accept that we have a choice. We can choose: *I am choosing my thoughts which are causing my anger. I can change my reaction to this event by changing how I think about it. I have the power to choose my emotions..*

My recognition of the need to maintain power over thoughts began with a book I read in 1982, *Erroneous Zones* (1976), by Dr. Wayne Dyer. In the book, Dr. Dyer offers ideas on taking charge of your thinking. Speaking of choosing how you feel, Dr. Dyer writes:

> *Feelings are not just emotions that happen to you. Feelings are reactions you choose to have. If you are in charge of your own emotions, you don't have to choose self-defeating reactions...*

Of taking charge of your thinking, Dyer adds: *This road will be new because you will see a given emotion as a choice rather than as a condition of life. This is the very heart and soul of personal freedom...* (p. 10)

Deliberate self-empowerment

If managing thoughts works to dispel negative emotions, then thoughts can certainly be used to empower positive ones. Say, for example, that we decide that we want to be more outspoken with friends. We can close our eyes and envision ourselves in a group situation with our friends. As we look upon that situation, we don't necessarily have to hear the words being spoken; we can simply observe and take note as we confidently exchange our opinions and ideas. We can observe as our friends in the imagined interaction respond favorably to our contribution. We can note the confidence on our faces as we speak. We can be proud of the genuine interest we show as we listen to others share their points of view. We can continue imagining this scenario for as long or as little as we like. Pulling together the thoughts and images needed for this imagined scenario is the first step in making the change we request. Adding the emotional component of confidence or pride increases the odds of success.

We can use this or similar techniques to deliberately choose to enhance whatever traits we wish to empower within us. Choosing, changing, and shaping our thoughts are strategies that serve us well on the path to self-discovery and empowerment.

Emotions, and how to heal and empower the true self

Our emotions are often indicators of the direction in which our thoughts are taking us. A negative thought system left unchecked can keep us from recognizing our innermost desires and purposes. Whenever we're immersed in negative emotions, we're less likely to be fully present in our interactions with others. At the same time, our *coping styles* and our *relationships* reflect the chaos that comes with altered perceptions. Our *self-concept* suffers if we allow ourselves to react based only on our emotions.

The good news is that we can use our power to change the channel (or other strategies in this chapter) and return to a more peaceful emotional state. With stress and negativity effectively silenced, we can tune in more easily to the true self's urges and nudges—a vital step in self-discovery and empowerment.

This chapter offers ideas and strategies for taking charge of your emotional state in a manner that will allow you to recognize your true self. Our experiences are unique. The following exercise may be helpful in stimulating self-examination with regard to your personal experience.

Exercise:

1. Describe how thoughts can lead to emotions.
2. Reflect on your emotional state. Have you felt any strong emotion, either negative or positive in the past month? If so, what specific self-talk could you have employed to change it?
3. Three people observe a child throwing a tantrum over not getting a candy bar. One observer is irritated because the mother won't stop the child from throwing a fit. Another observer is looking at the child and begins to feel overwhelmed with sadness. The third observer is feeling compassion for the mother. What are the root causes of the different reactions?
4. What possible thoughts might each observer have in #3 above? What specific thoughts could change the emotional state of the first two observers?
5. What strategy have you used in the past for changing your emotions/thoughts?
6. Thinking back over the ideas in this chapter, what new strategy are you willing to try?

The meeting of two personalities is like the contact
of two chemical substances: if there is any reaction,
both are transformed.

—Carl Gustav Jung (1875-1961)

Chapter Eight - Being Fully Present in Relationships

Working with couples in counseling offers some unique dynamics to consider. A typical first session involves one person or the other (or both) detailing a long list of what the other person does wrong. At some point during that session, I will say something like this:

*The only person you can really change is you. You can't change your partner. Only your partner can do that. Counseling for you will involve **you** looking at what **you** do to contribute to the problems that **you** have been telling me about. Even if your partner never changes, if you change the way you respond to your partner, the potential is there for everything to change.*

The bottom line is that improving relationships requires increased self-awareness and knowledge of the dynamics that can impair our perceptions, and perceptions are so often skewed by the internalization of our past experiences.

In the preceding chapters, we learned that when we are in a highly charged emotional state, we risk regressing or collapsing into the past, that is, a part of us is not fully present and is allowing unfinished business from the past to interfere with the present. When this is occurring, we are definitely not fully present. When I see couples or families regarding problems, it's very rare for the family NOT to have high levels of emotion. It is only logical, then, that one of our first tasks in therapy is to work deliberately on staying in the present moment.

He said, she said…

It still amazes me that two people can be in the same situation, at the same time, and yet have two totally different stories of what happened. Both are telling what they believe is the truth. When this comes up in counseling, it's usually over an important matter, a matter where someone's ego is on the line. Eventually, as the argument ensues, I find that both parties are looking to me to choose sides. I usually say something less than profound like "I believe both of you," and I say that with all due respect to the situation. You see, I know that our perceptions create (and distort) our respective realities, so, when this kind of situation comes up, I know that at least one person's version is distorted. Nevertheless, both are telling the truth as they see it. Neither will back down. There will be no compromise. And, at this point, there is no point in pursuing the matter. Usually, I will have both restate their position and acknowledge each other's. And that's about as good as it gets—until we get further along in counseling. If they stay in counseling, the couple will learn to recognize all the dynamics involved in their interactions. They will become less reactive and more pensive.

About Grace

Recall the story of Grace and how she was able to rid herself of headaches. Early in counseling, Grace determined that her relationships were out of balance. In other words, she was doing too much of the work of the relationships. She was carrying the load. If she sensed conflict, she would go into peacemaker mode. If she sensed disapproval from others, she would self-blame. This same scenario played out in the division of chores and household responsibilities. Grace was good! She could do it all. She was super-woman, super-wife, super-mom, and super-employee! The only relationship she neglected was her relationship with herself.

Grace realized early that her relationship with her two children and her husband would need to change for Grace to get better. Before she could make any real strides, however, she had to find and give a voice to her true self. Finding the voice was not a problem for Grace, as she had very good intuition. She *knew* what she had to do but had a difficult time finding the courage and strength to do it. When attempting to put into action what she *knew* she had to do, Grace asked two questions that I hear very often as a counselor:

- Why can't I say what I know I need to say?
- Why can't I do what I know I need to do?

When I hear those kinds of "why questions," I know that there is something afoot at the unconscious level, the source of which my client and I might never discover. It's usually a powerful force requiring conscious effort to overcome and transform. I've come to believe that this force relates to shadow dynamics based on at least one of these two issues:

- the sum total of inherited generational dysfunction and/or
- the workings of a wounded and disoriented inner child

In Grace's case, both forces were at work. Grace had grown up in a home where domestic violence was present. Grace watched as her father dominated, belittled, and physically harmed her mother. Grace learned the importance of watching for moods and reading between the lines. At an early age, Grace had become hyper-vigilant of others' needs. She believed that if she could make someone feel better that she (and her mother) could be safe. So, beginning at about age two, Grace committed to what became a lifelong coping style, i.e., to do whatever it took to avoid conflict. This meant that she had to keep others happy, regardless of what her intuition told her. Grace learned how to survive in relationships, that the male dominates and the female accepts her situation without complaint. Grace's inner child, the part of her that observed the relationship dynamics, held tightly to her beliefs to keep others happy. In fact, everyone in Grace's sphere of influence was content, except for Grace. The point is that all of Grace's striving to please others required her to ignore the voice of her true self while using a coping mechanism she had learned as a very young child. To further complicate matters, Grace communicated *indirectly,* which required others to figure out what she really meant. Because she wasn't always clear, Grace often didn't get what she wanted – something that caused growing resentment in her closest relationships.

Through signs and intuition, Grace began to feel that her husband was cheating on her. Grace's fear of conflict kept her from addressing her husband's infidelity even as the evidence and her suspicions mounted. Repressing this issue required an enormous amount of energy resulting in Grace's depleted physical resources—a state that eventually resulted in her headaches.

When I met Grace, her true self was exhausted, deeply sad, and on the verge of giving up on life. After all, her true self had endured years of helping others with little or no effort put into development and empowerment of the self.

If you were to ask Grace today the answer to those two questions: *Why can't I say what I need to say? Why can't I do what I need to do?* she would know the answer. Grace came to recognize that it was her inner child that was making adult relationship decisions, not the responsible adult that she was. It was Grace's inner child that communicated a paralyzing fear whenever there was a potential for conflict. Rather than ignore the feelings of fear, Grace gave in to them. But no more. Today, when Grace feels the fear, she gives it her attention, but in a different way. Today, Grace knows that many of her automatic responses are related to what she learned about relationships from her parents. She also recognizes that there is still a very young part of her that needs to feel safe. Today, within a few seconds of the onset of a negative emotion, Grace allows herself to envision a very young Grace. She mentally approaches this image of herself and embraces her, assuring her that she will keep her safe, that she is an adult now and can make good choices.

Grace remains fully present when she listens to and follows her intuition. This prevents her from being sidetracked by the despair and fear of her wounded inner child. Grace now has the capability to be fully present in all of her relationships. Grace would be the first one to say that being fully present is not easy, but the rewards are well worth the effort.

Maintaining present moment clarity in the face of triggers

As with Grace, it is within our closest relationships that we do the work of intimacy. This is because it was in our earliest, more intimate relationships that we made decisions about who and how to be.

You and I have everything to gain and nothing to lose by

staying in the present, especially when interactions with others are involved. Odds are improved for present-moment clarity when our level of self awareness includes the knowledge of our personal issues and triggers. (If you've made it this far in the book but haven't completed the shadow exercise, stop here and do it now. Go back to Chapter Four to find the exercise.) With the aid of information garnered through that exercise we can transform our relationships by reaching new levels of intimacy and trust from what we learn about ourselves. In the exercise, we identified many of our personal triggers (button pushing traits). When interacting with someone, if one of those identified traits or actions is displayed by us or by the other person, we are at high risk *not* to be in the present moment. It's in our best interest to memorize our shadow risks and to carry the knowledge of them with us at all times.

Triggers are often highly personalized, that is, what triggers one person may not necessarily trigger another. For example, let's say that a father had to work every Saturday growing up, preventing him from attending his son's Little League ball games. The odds are high, then, that the son (as an adult) will over-react to an announcement from his wife that she has volunteered to work on Saturdays for the next three months. If the son/husband expresses irritation and anger over his wife's choice to volunteer, she is likely not to understand. With an escalated emotional state, odds are that the son/husband is not fully present within this interaction. In this example, self-awareness and clarity are important. If the son/husband can recognize that he has an unresolved childhood issue related to an important person in his life not being available on Saturdays, he can proceed cautiously through his interactions with his wife about Saturday volunteering. The caution for him involves testing his thoughts and statements for truth and healthy assertion while managing his emotions.

When we are triggered, we are not fully present. Instead, we are reacting to any number of past hurts or fears. To gain command of our present moment, we employ strategies to eliminate or reduce the impact of our triggers on us and our relationships.

Potential trigger-tripping *words and phrases*

Even though triggers are personal, there are some common trigger-tripping words and phrases. When we eliminate our use of these (and temper our response to them), we greatly improve the odds of staying fully present in our interactions.

Here are a few common words and phrases:

- Why? (when used as a question about a personal behavior or thought)
- Why not?
- Why did you….?
- Why didn't you…?
- You should have…
- You shouldn't have…
- You always…
- You never…

These words and phrases imply judgment and are experienced by the other party in the exchange as criticism and, at a deeper level, as an effort to control. When two people in a close relationship use these kinds of phrases, separation is the result. The image that the use of these words conjures up for me is of one person pointing his (or her) finger while the other bows down or points back. I think that you'll agree that this does not foster intimacy. Think of all the potential unresolved childhood issues that this pointing image suggests: being corrected by a teacher, observing domestic violence, being challenged or disciplined, being criticized and misunderstood, to name a few. Regressing back to the emotional state of a young child will only serve to complicate the interaction.

Feelings of unworthiness, shame, anger, hurt, betrayal, and many more are triggered with the use of these and similar words. When I see this dynamic in couples that I work with, I give them an assignment to immediately ban the use of these phrases and to have a non-verbal signal to remind each other when one of these phrases is used. These phrases, deeply ingrained into our communication and coping styles, cripple our attempts to remain present in our interactions.

There are other, more gentle ways to say what we need to say. One key to authentic and less conflict-laden communication is to express *what we want*, not *what the other person should or should not do or be*, etc. So, if we are hurt and disappointed with our spouse for being late for a special dinner, rather than saying, *"Why were you late?"*, instead we can be completely truthful: *"I feel hurt and disappointed that you didn't make it home on time."* The latter is much more difficult to articulate when in strong emotion, but it's less likely to trigger the other person and more likely to be acknowledged.

Potential trigger-tripping *actions:*

The items in this list contain actions (and inactions) that can trip triggers between people who care about each other.

- Using a loud voice
- Disrespectful communications (cursing, labeling, name-calling, using sarcasm, etc.)
- Not acknowledging the other person
- Not responding to inquiries
- Hostile or angry body language
- Interrupting

The above actions can easily trigger other people, causing them to regress to a time when they were hurt by distancing or by being confronted. These actions can certainly lead to conflict or complete avoidance of conflict. Neither is fruitful in resolving the issue, which likely calls for healthy coping skills.

Potential trigger-laden *topics:*

- Money issues
- Religious and political differences

- Opinions about family and extended family
- Children
- Sex
- Any potential disagreement

If you are involved in a heated discussion that involves any of the above, beware! If any of these issues were played out in an unhealthy fashion in your childhood, you are at risk to regress back to your parents' coping style (or the extreme opposite). Often, with couples that I have seen, one of them usually says, "My parents never argued." This person will often dislike conflict and believe that something is wrong with the partner who challenges his or her actions or opinions. They're likely to say things like "It's not worth fighting about." Usually, the other party in this relationship grew up in a vocal family where strong opinions were expressed. Sometimes the arguments got out of hand, sometimes not, but, regardless, there's one party with no experience with conflict in a relationship with a person who is well-versed in expressing his or her opinion. Both must learn to be in the present moment and to honor each other's experience, without judging it as right or wrong.

Tools for staying fully present

Here are two things you can do now to improve your odds of staying fully present in any kind of interaction:

1. Listen completely.
2. Maintain non-threatening and open body language

Listen completely

Listening is one of the greatest gifts you can give to those you love. Good listening skills in relationships lead to greater understanding by all parties, for all parties. Good listening promotes and enhances intimacy.

Whether I am working with a couple or with individuals, there are at least three basic communication skills learned and practiced within the counseling setting.

- Reflective listening
- Paraphrasing
- I-messages

Below is a brief description and discussion of these three skills, all of which can be important in-the-moment aids for remaining fully present.

Reflective listening is a form of listening that requires the listener to listen for the *feeling* underneath the speaker's words and to *reflect that feeling* back to the speaker using phrases with words like *sounds like you feel….* or *seems like you feel…*

Here is an example of potentially *ineffective* listening:

Joe: "I am sick and tired of doing everyone else's work. I end up staying late while everyone else gets to go home and be with their family."

Mary: "It's time you found another job."

Joe: "We've talked about this before. I don't want to quit my job!"

Here's a more effective approach involving reflective listening. Notice the difference in Joe's response.

Joe: "I am sick and tired of doing everyone else's work. I end up staying late while everyone else gets to go home and be with their family."

Mary: "You sound really frustrated."

Joe: "I *am* frustrated, and angry. Maybe I need to talk with my boss."

In the second example, Mary reflected what she believed was Joe's feeling: frustration. In the example, she was on target. But, if she had been wrong, odds are, Joe would have said something like "Well not *frustrated*, just really *down* about a seemingly impossible situation." Using reflective listening sends an underlying message of *I care about you* that is received regardless of the accuracy of your statement. In fact, Joe had to look within himself at his own emotions to verify that Mary was accurate before responding. This gave him a chance to examine his own feelings and possibly to consider how he was coming across. What I've noticed when couples practice reflective listening in counseling is that people tend to project their own feelings on to the other person—which is sometimes accurate and sometimes very off target. Using reflective listening is a win-win situation. It keeps us from regressing into our own issues by focusing on the other person's feelings. In addition, reflective listening helps the other person stay present by having them look within to find their feelings and express them.

Paraphrasing

Paraphrasing is a simple tool that can make a huge difference. To paraphrase another party, simply restate the words that the other person spoke in a tentative fashion. It can help to use this starter sentence stem:

So, you are saying…
Using the situation between Joe and Mary, here's an example of using paraphrasing:

Joe: "I am sick and tired of doing everyone else's work. I end up staying late while everyone else gets to go home and be with their family."

Mary: "*So, you are saying* that you are tired of staying late doing everybody's work, while they go home to be with their families? (paraphrasing)

Joe: "Yes. In fact, yesterday Ted actually called me from home to make sure I finished his module before I left!"

Mary: "You sound really irritated." (reflective listening)

There will be more discussion of the importance of paraphrasing later in this chapter.

I-messages

I-messages provide a way to express feelings and thoughts in an assertive, non-threatening manner. I-messages have a minimum of two parts. Here are the stems:

I feel _____ when you _____.

Let's say that Mary doesn't like Joe coming in late. It leaves her with all the household responsibilities like cooking and cleaning. Mary can use an I-message to state her concerns:

Mary: "When you're unable to get home in time to help me around the house, I feel discouraged."

Notice that Mary is citing Joe's behavior (coming in late) only. I-messages do a good job of separating the "deed from the doer." In other words, instead of accusing Joe of being discouraging, she focuses on the specific behavior.

Some books and articles on I-messages support the use of adding a "because" phrase. This can be used but requires even more skill. If we are going to use "because," never follow it with the word "you."

Here's how it can go wrong. Watch how it turns into a lecture.

When you are unable to get home on time to help around the house, **I feel** *discouraged **because you** never come home on time and you never think about how hard it is to have to work all day, take care of supper and cleaning before I can even sit down and relax.*

If, instead of following the *because* with *you*, follow it with *I* and see what happens. Notice the difference below:

When you are unable to get home on time to help around the house, **I feel** discouraged ***because I** am tired when I get home.*

In summary, when using I-messages, caution is necessary if using a *because*. I-messages generally address problematic situations with conflict potential. Careful consideration and choice of words assists in reducing the risk of triggers. I-messages allow us to make our point about a problematic behavior without putting down the other person.

Maintain open and non-threatening body language

Actively working on the image we present during interactions can make noticeable differences in the effectiveness of our communications.

DO:
- Maintain eye contact
- Keep a relaxed body posture.
- Display an interested or concerned facial expression.
- Lean slightly forward.
- Focus only on the message.

DON'T:
- Cross your arms.
- Make a fist.
- Look away.
- Begin to formulate a response. (It shows on your facial expression.)
- Position yourself physically above the other person.
- Lean away or put your feet up.
- Tend to your cell phone.
- Walk away.

Taking these steps will reduce the odds of one or both parties regressing into the past and losing touch with the present moment.

A great source of information with our communication skills can be our friends. We can elicit their support by letting them know that we are working on healthy self-expression. We can ask for feedback about our communication style, especially any negative verbal or non-verbal mannerisms that they have observed.

Hear the words only

There is one very common problem that I have noticed with the way we humans, in general, communicate. We tend not to take people at face value; that is, we tend to hear what the person is saying, then we wonder if they really mean it or we decide what it is they really mean. We don't allow others to be accountable for their words. If we are interpreting, analyzing, and changing their message, then how can we hold them accountable for what we hear? We hold them accountable when we react to what we think they meant. The best way to debunk this very messy and extremely common way of communicating is to hear and respond solely to the person's words.

When I began to ask couples within counseling sessions to use paraphrasing, I was shocked by how often inaccurate interpretation occurred within relationships as well as how much chaos was caused by the interpretations.

Note the interpretation occurring in the following examples of some failed paraphrasing attempts. The appropriate paraphrasing response *in italics* comes immediately after the interpretation to illustrate the difference.

Joe: I was embarrassed when you called my friend to check up on me.

Mary: So you are saying you are mad at me?
       So you are saying you were embarrassed?

Joe: What I need from you are signs of affection.

Mary: So you are saying that I never show you any signs of affection?
       So you are saying you need signs of affection from me?

Joe: When you didn't call me back, I was worried.

Mary: So, you are saying that you expect me to call you back
         within five minutes of when you leave me a message?
         *So you are saying you were worried when I didn't call you
         back?*

In the above examples, it's easy to see how the interpretations could easily lead to conflict or inner turmoil for one or more parties.

One assignment I give to my clients that helps to debunk this problem is to *hear only the words* of the other party. This sounds simple, but it is one of the most difficult assignments for clients to accomplish. We are so used to reading into each other's facial expressions, body postures, tones of voice, etc., that we often give more value to the non-verbal aspects of communication. By agreeing to hear only the words, the pressure is on the person who wants to communicate his or her needs clearly, rather than the listener to interpret them.

There are so many benefits to the technique of hearing only the words. No longer do I hear from my clients that the other party should've known what they were feeling or what is the person wanted.

People and patterns

Looking back on our pasts and our relationships, many of us might find that we tend to attract friends that have similar characteristics. For example, do we tend to attract people who think they know everything and like to tell us what to do? If so, it's possible that we draw these people to us because of our own insecurities and/or our inability to speak our truths. The point is that if we have an unhealthy pattern, there's likely a clue within the pattern that suggests opportunity for change.

Let's take a look at the relationships, patterns, and clues of the clients we have met in this book:

Grace

Grace's pattern in friendships was to attract friends with bossy personalities. She would often get their opinions on important matters and follow their opinions without regard for her own. She saw herself as weak and insecure. As Grace learned to speak her truth, she fortified herself. In so doing, she did not lose all of her friends—just the ones that could no longer boss her around. Her other relationships deepened as a result of mutual respect. Grace's old pattern was a clue to her that she needed to develop her "bossiness" (which we discovered was simply her speaking her truth). Her new pattern is to attract people into her life that are more balanced.

Joey

Joey carried his unresolved history of abuse and neglect into his relationships. Joey's pattern was to attract others whom he eventually perceived as being hurtful and abandoning his needs (abusive and neglectful). Joey's choice to stop looking for and collecting evidence of abuse and neglect cleared the air and made space for a new pattern in relationships, one in which he allowed himself to believe that others enjoyed his company. The important clue in Joey's old pattern was his hypervigilance for signs of potential hurt and abandonment.

Celeste

Recall that everyone loved Celeste! The people she called friends when she started counseling were those that looked up to her and admired her. While this sounds positive, keep in mind that a true friend is willing to tell you when you are not perfect and will help you with your blind spots. Her pattern of drawing admirers to her was keeping her from developing her own sense of self. It was as if these admirers became an addiction for her. Her old, recurring pattern was a clue to her that she needed to develop some self-admiration. Her new and more successful pattern is to attract people based on the criteria of similar beliefs, values, interests, and activities.

Breaking patterns

It's in the recognition of the pattern that healing begins. Think of a watch as having a definite pattern and predictable movements.

If you were to extract just one tiny part from the inner workings of a watch, it wouldn't work. It's the same with breaking relationship patterns. Identifying one small part of the damaging pattern and changing it creates an opportunity for potential change in the overall pattern.

Here are some questions to consider if a pattern is present:

- What is the pattern? What are the details of the pattern?
- What is the exact opposite of the pattern that I'm attracting?
- Does the opposite pattern represent a healing opportunity for me?
- Am I attracting people to me that treat me the way I treat myself?
- If this person is in my life to teach me a lesson in personal growth, what is the lesson?

Patterns hold clues for us to change the pattern. Find the clue. Make the change. Break the pattern.

Integrity in relationships

Applying the ideas in this chapter enhances our integrity with ourselves, as well as with others. Intimacy grows from the increased trust that follows reduced reactivity and improved listening skills.

Within counseling, my clients often develop their own checklist based on the ideas in this chapter that pertain to them. Below is an example of a checklist that someone working on relationships might create. Completing this checklist is a reminder of a commitment to the relationship as well as an intention to stay in the present moment. Each list is different based on the needs of the client and/ or the relationship. This has proven to be a very successful tool in raising awareness and changing unhealthy patterns.

Daily Relationship Integrity Checklist							
Week of:	**M**	**T**	**W**	**T**	**F**	**S**	**S**
I showed signs of affection.							
I used a respectful tone of voice.							
My facial expression and body language was positive or neutral.							
I hugged my spouse in the morning and upon returning from work.							
I said goodnight or good-by when appropriate.							
I spoke my truth today.							
I used my listening skills today.							
I monitored my emotional state.							
I examined my reactions to determine if I was fully present or regressing.							
I verbally answered all questions.							
I did not use the word "Why."							
I did not use the word "Should."							
I did not criticize.							

Relationships, and how to heal and empower the true self

Our ability to stay true to our self can be sorely tested within relationships. Since many of our childhood wounds occurred within a primary relationship, we are at high risk to react inappropriately within our closest *relationships*. When we are triggered, our *coping styles* are often driven by old, unresolved pain. Allowing ourselves to be triggered can often have painful consequences which, if repeated often enough, can affect our *self-concept*. Our relationships are enhanced by our ability to stay connected to our true selves. Staying in the present moment by using the strategies and ideas in this chapter ensures integrity in all of our relationships. Staying fully present in relationships provides opportunities for self-discovery and empowerment.

Exercise

1. What is meant by the phrase "being fully present in relationships"? How can being fully present help relationships? How can it help you?
2. Can you think of a time in the past when you acted like one of your parents? Can you think of a time when you acted in the opposite way?
3. What is a trigger? Think of a time when you were triggered. Think about a time when someone else was triggered and how it affected your communication and your relationship.
4. What trigger-tripping words or phrases do you use? What words and phrases trigger you?
5. What body language do you use when you are angry? When you are confronted? When you are asking for something?
6. What is the purpose of reflective listening and paraphrasing? How can it help your relationships?
7. What is the purpose of I-messages?
8. If you're not completely convinced that being fully present in relationships requires increased awareness of your own triggers, re-read the Shadow chapter and this chapter. If you

haven't done the Shadow exercise, do it now! It helps you to identify your triggers and your risks in relationships.

9. Dedicate some time observing others and watching for triggers and problematic communication styles.

10. Ask your partner, your friends, and your family for feedback on your communication style.

11. Next time someone is angry with you, try reflective listening and watch how it seems to defuse the level of emotion.

12. Make your own **Integrity Checklist** to match your specific needs.

This above all: to thine own self be true…

—William Shakespeare

Chapter Nine - Speaking the Truth

When we listen to and voice the subtle communications of our true selves, we are speaking our truths. When we say what we know we need to say and we speak up in spite of our fear of conflict or judgment, we are speaking our truth. Ignoring our truth risks making choices and decisions that distance us from what it is we really want to do and how we desire to be. Not speaking our truths prevents important people in our lives from knowing us completely. Not speaking our truths is a subtle form of dishonesty.

We have within us the ability to know when we are living our lives in a manner consistent with our truths. Likewise, we can sense when we are not speaking our truths. In this chapter, we discuss how to recognize our truths as well as the importance of speaking them.

Physical sensation of the truth

Our truths are always available to us. Yet sometimes, within our present moment, our truths can be difficult to access. This is often due to the psychological noise that exudes from a stressed physical or emotional state.

One very reliable indicator of whether or not you, your words, or your actions are being consistent with your true self is found in your body. If you have ever been around a small child that tells a lie, you probably recall how his whole body seemed to cringe and to fight telling the lie. Like a small child, I believe that no matter what age we are, our body and all of our senses resist any time we express ourselves in a manner not consistent with our true selves. It appears that as we get older, we get better at tuning out these important signals that seem to be built in at birth.

Your physical experience of these signals may be unique for you. For me, if I distort the truth in any fashion, I feel as if a hole has opened in my heart and energy is pouring out of me. Others report that they feel sick to the stomach when they are dishonest. Still others say they feel tension in their heads, throats, necks, and backs if they are not acting or speaking with integrity. Imagine the effect on your body and spirit if day in and day out, you are unable to say what you need to say or be who you want to be!

Here's an exercise that's helpful in gaining awareness about the physical sensations that naturally occur when we speak anything but the truth:

1. Find a place where you can speak aloud freely and privately.
2. Get comfortable. Take a few long, slow, deep breaths to prepare for this exercise.
3. Think of something important to you and make up a lie about it.
4. *Tell the lie* to yourself *out loud*, repeating it until you begin to feel the uncomfortable sensations that accompany it.
5. Note where you feel the conflict. You may feel the conflict in more than one area of your body or in one area more strongly than in other areas. Each affected area is a potential true-self indicator.
6. Now, tell the truth about the issue, and notice as the tension and resistance changes in those same areas of your body.
7. Resolve to listen to your body as you move throughout your daily routine.

Meditation and the truth

Meditation is a great noise reduction tool. While meditation is not required for us to know our truth, it can greatly enhance our ability to connect with it. Meditation has been shown to reduce stress, improve health (including reverse heart disease), reduce physical pain, and improve the immune system. In addition, meditation involves thought control, a skill that greatly enhances our ability to remain in the present moment as we move through the day-to-day activities of our lives.

Meditating regularly enables us to be more mindful of our

emotions and the reactions within our bodies. In tune with these sensations, we can use them to access our truths and make corrections when we find ourselves out of sync with them.

Grace and her truth

Let's take a look at Grace again. At work, Grace was perceived as being a hard worker, always willing to volunteer and help others. Grace developed physical and emotional problems because she overly identified with those traits to the point of negation of her true self. From day one in counseling, Grace's true self seemed to be shouting "NO, *I do not want to live like this anymore!*" As Grace got better, she set boundaries at work. If she did not have time for committee assignments, she'd say no without hesitation. If Grace had other things she preferred to do, she wouldn't stay late to help others.

Do people think less of Grace now? Absolutely not. In fact, Grace is more respected now than ever before. Today, Grace is still described as a hard worker, willing to volunteer and help others *but also someone whom you can trust to speak her truth and say what is on her mind.* What has happened at work is that Grace no longer carries around an extra load of resentment and anger at others. She is more cheerful and pleasant. The workload is more evenly distributed and, in fact, there is a spirit of teamwork that wasn't apparent prior to Grace making her own personal changes.

Please note that Grace did not go to the extreme and start saying NO to everything. Today, Grace says yes to some assignments and no to others. She continues to actively strive to live in a balanced manner. She remains balanced by tuning in to her truth and speaking it in a kind but firm manner.

Speaking our truths in day-to-day situations

Once we have learned to tune in to our truths, we can assess how we express our truths in our daily interactions with others.

Here are a few questions to consider.

- Are our actions, choices, and statements consistent with our internal reality?
- Do we attempt to redefine ourselves based on other people's apparent needs?
- Do we hesitate to express an opinion because we know the other person has a different one?
- Do we allow fear of judgment or condemnation to keep our true self-expression at bay?
- Do we inadvertently push people away with our abrasiveness?

It isn't necessary to share everything about ourselves with everyone. This would lead to vulnerability. Likewise, it's not critical to self-development that we always express our opinions when called upon. As in all things, achievement of balance is the key.

What is balanced self-expression? It involves sharing our opinions, while also accepting that others may also have their own. In doing so, we are acknowledging our truth while at the same time allowing space for the other party to express his or hers. If we become opinionated and always perceive that we are right, then we alienate others who can sense the shadow energy (too much opinion) and, as a result, begin to negate our opinion. If we allow others' opinions to always have precedence over our own, we are once again at one end of the shadow see-saw, out of balance, and vulnerable to others' beliefs and perceptions, which can be just as distorted as ours.

The folly of never considering another's opinion is illustrated in Hans Christian Andersen's tale, *The Emperor's New Clothes* (1837). In that tale, the Emperor is convinced by two trickster tailors that they have invented a new fabric that only *stupid* people cannot see. He goes on parade to show off this beautiful fabric. As a child shouts, "*The emperor is naked,*" others join in. But the Emperor, hanging on to his belief that those who do not see his clothes are stupid, holds his head high and continues the parade.

None of us would willingly want to be the Emperor. Others' opinions can give us important feedback about ourselves. The key is to listen to the feedback, take a look at whether or not we can accept it as true, and then decide if changes are necessary. If the matter is significant and involves important aspects of ourselves, including those of character, we may want to elicit additional feedback from others.

Honest feedback from others is important for our growth. Much of this book has discussed how our past experiences affect our perceptions and actions in the present moment. Other people can help us by being a mirror for us. A good friend with the courage to tell us that we are wrong is a good friend indeed. We must be aware, however, that we aren't the only one affected by life's experiences. Our good friend, then, could be wrong. The bottom line involves your ability to connect with your truth. And, once we find it, we live it and express it with confidence.

An in-the-moment, self-preserving strategy

When others share something negative about us to us, something with which we don't agree, there's substantial risk for an emotional or triggered response. In other words, we may react angrily out of hurt or we may not be able to say what we want to say out of fear of conflict. In both cases, the true self is not being adequately asserted.

A tried and true strategy for self-preservation in the middle of a difficult moment, involves *acknowledging what the other person said* and then *stating that you will give that idea some thought*.

Note the increasing level of assertiveness in the following examples:

> *I hear you saying that you think I'm selfish. I'll give that some thought.*
>
> *I hear you saying that you think I'm selfish. I disagree, but I'll think about what you said.*
>
> *I hear you saying that you think I'm selfish. I disagree, but I'll think about what you said and get back with you.*

This simple strategy allows us to preserve the right to our own opinions while still considering the opinions of others. We buy time, without reacting. Our duty to ourselves is to go within at our earliest convenience, check out the truth of the other person's statement and then act accordingly.

Speaking our truths to others about them

Caution is warranted when we decide to speak our (negative) truth *about* others *to* them! In the case of the Emperor, the opinion of a young child that the emperor is naked is not enough to sway him, nor is the murmur of the crowd. However, imagine if those who were closest to him sat him down, looked him in the eye and said with compassion: *Emperor, these men are tricksters and thieves. None of us has been able to see the fabric. Trust us, we care about you. Don't go on parade.*

We don't have an obligation to other people to set them straight about themselves, yet if we care about them, do we allow them to experience consequences because we failed to speak up? The answer to that question varies based on the person, the situation, and the risks involved.

One thing to consider before we offer our opinion is that the issue we wish to speak to the other person about may be our own. Very often as I listen to a client describe the negative traits of someone else, I realize that the words being spoken are actually words that the client needs to hear. For example, I recall a client who told me that his wife talked too much and never listened to him. In the process of that session and many that followed, it became clear that the husband talked entirely too much and rarely acknowledged the few statements that I made.

Sharing negative information can trigger shadow states. Some may perceive the information as criticism, while others perceive it as judgment or arrogance. Still others may see it for what it is, a gesture of friendship based on a friend's perception. The higher the level of intimacy and trust in the relationship, the more likely the message will be heard. However, in a potentially damaging turn of events, if the other person places too much trust in us, they may give our opinions and observations too much power while neglecting to consider their own. It's wise to temper our own certainty with humility. Too much certainty in any message can be perceived as judgment or arrogance. If this happens, credibility is lost and misunderstandings result!

If, after serious consideration, you feel the need to share negative information to another, go forward in this manner:

1. Look within to consider if there is a shadow dynamic trying to pull you (and your friend) into your own issues.
2. If so, you can reassess the message to see if it's valid for your friend too. If not, stop here.
3. You can ask yourself if the message will empower the other person. If not, consider the importance and necessity of the information before proceeding.
4. You can consider if the person will accept your truth as his or her own without self-evaluation. If not, then don't proceed.
5. You can consider if the person will be receptive to feedback about the issue. If not, then don't proceed.
6. If, after considering all of the above, you decide to continue, you can preface the discussion with a statement that what you are saying is just to be *considered*, i.e., that he or she must find his or her own truth. Work to balance certainty with an equal amount of humility.
7. At this point, you have spoken your truth and can let go of the outcome.

If, after reviewing the above list, you still feel the need to comment, the best bet for being heard involves the deliberate placement of compassion in your voice and eyes as you proceed. Once you have spoken, it is best not to be too invested in the outcome. You are speaking your truth and that's all that's happening. Depending upon the response, it can help the situation and the relationship to ask for feedback from the person about what you've just said and the information you've shared.

The person likely needs time to go within and determine if what you've said is true. Using the emperor example, he may need some alone time in front of a mirror to accept that he was duped and that there really are no clothes. It may take the emperor a while to unravel the belief system that had him order the clothes in the first place. Similarly, it may take your friend a while to consider what you've said.

Even if you've reviewed all the aspects of the above points before sharing the information, it's very possible that you may later realize that the issue you talked about to the friend was actually an issue related to yourself.

In his book, *The Road Less Traveled*, M. Scott Peck, M. D. discusses a life dedicated to the truth. He says: *Courageous people, must continually push themselves to be completely honest, yet must also possess the capacity to withhold the truth when appropriate. (pg. 64)*

There are times when we do not have an option but to speak our truths to others regardless of the potential outcome. In these cases, the problems are very serious and intervention may be needed, as with addictions, serious mental disorders, etc.

Speaking truth, and how to heal and empower the true self

In summary, we begin to heal and empower the true self by gaining access to our truths. We will find it easier to access our truths when we are able to get in touch with the physical and emotional sensations that accompany the expression of truth and non-truth. Speaking our truths within our interactions with others improves our *self-concepts*, because we are living in a way that is consistent with who we are. Speaking our truths improves *relationships* by keeping them in the present moment. It also keeps us from playing roles or games within relationships. Speaking our truths is a self-empowering *coping style*.

Finally, we should use caution when sharing negative information about others to them. There is high risk that we are projecting our own traits onto the other person. *If in doubt about what you have to say and your motivation*, don't share.

This chapter contains a few examples of ways in which we can connect with and speak our truths within relationships. Remember that your experience is uniquely yours. The following exercise may be helpful in stimulating your thinking with regard to your experience.

Exercise:

1. Do you speak your truth? At work? At home? With certain people but not others?
2. Are you abrasive when you speak your truth? Do you speak your truth too passively?
3. What difference would it make in your relationships with the above people if you did speak your truth?
4. Pay attention to patterns. Do you find yourself wanting to comment on the same issue with different people? For example, do you regularly tend to comment on other people's laziness or irresponsibility? If so, what does this say about you? Are you lazy, irresponsible or perhaps too industrious and overly-responsible?
5. Are you having problems finding compassion for others when you speak your truth about them? If so, consider how compassionate you are toward yourself.
6. How do you react when others give you "constructive criticism"? What does your reaction say about you?
7. How is the true self empowered by speaking the truth in an effective manner?

Love is an act of endless forgiveness, a tender look which becomes a habit.

—Peter Ustinov

Chapter Ten - Forgiving Yourself and Others

Resentment, bitterness, anger and hurt interfere with the connection to our true selves. Ruminating over wrongs and clinging to negative emotions will tighten the bond to the past, keeping us from fully experiencing the present. Practicing forgiveness dissolves these emotions while creating a space for greater intimacy in relationships. In this chapter we take a comprehensive look at forgiveness, expanding its meaning broadly to maximize opportunities for healing.

Forgiving others

The words *I forgive you*, while worthy, represent just a small part of the forgiveness process. Complete forgiveness involves a process that can span months and even years. Compassion is an important aspect of the forgiveness process. While forgiveness is the ultimate goal, compassion is the means to achieve that goal.

True and complete forgiveness involves the following processes:

1. Find understanding and compassion for the person, persons, or situation.
2. Learn to manage actions and reactions to the person or situation.
3. Determine personal responsibility, if any, to avoid repeating the situation.
4. Bring compassion to the person, situation, and ourselves.

Find understanding and compassion

Being wronged does not feel good. Emotions ranging from rage to deep hurt can surface when we have been hurt by someone. The stronger the tie to the person, the stronger the emotional reaction will be. Recall Grace's situation. When Grace overcame her fear of conflict and dared to approach her husband with the issue of his cheating, she initially expressed extreme anger. She resorted to name-calling and insults. For example, the other woman was *easy*, while her husband was a *cheat and liar*. These statements falsely empowered Grace to feel temporarily in control but, in actuality, were part of a coping style she had learned from childhood. Grace's anger prevented her from feeling authentic feelings of hurt and sadness while putting more and more distance between herself and her husband. For Grace to begin forgiving, she had to seek understanding and compassion for her husband and his choice to have an affair.

This is not easy work. Whether it is you, me, or Grace, when we've been wronged it's very difficult to reverse the negative emotions once they begin to spiral downward. But it's not impossible! The reversal begins with a decision to counteract that emotion with understanding and compassion.

One strategy that sets the stage for compassion involves separating the deed from the doer. In other words, we can learn to recognize that the action does not define the person who did the hurting. The action or choice was wrong—not the person. If, for example, our boss chooses to promote someone over us, this does not mean he is an unfair and heartless person. Instead, the boss has made a choice (his deed), a choice that resulted in pain for us. We can choose to be frustrated with the boss' choice, not the boss as a human being. How we choose to react to a situation can make a big difference for us in the future.

Grace opened the door to compassion when she recognized that her husband was likely having a reaction to his own past when he had the affair. This reaction prevented him from being fully present and making a healthy decision. Grace separated the deed from the doer when she didn't allow her initial identification of her husband as a cheater to dictate her actions. At the time of the affair, Grace was working in counseling on being fully present. She chose to see her husband's actions of cheating as that of a hurting child, a child that desperately needed attention and admiration from others. The deed was wrong. To Grace, the doer (her husband) was a hurting child.

Changing how we think about a person involves being able to come up with alternate explanations. People make poor choices because of bad information, faulty perception, childhood wounds, inability to foresee the impact of the decision, addictions, etc. If we can allow an alternate explanation to emerge for the wrong that was done to us, we have successfully begun to reverse the downward spiral. Forgiveness is the goal. Think of compassion as the means to that end.

So, if Grace can forgive her husband, does that mean she needs to stay with him? That decision is a totally separate matter. In the end, Grace looked within and knew that she would have to live with her decision if she left him. Rather than leave abruptly, Grace arranged for couple counseling for herself and her husband. When counseling was unsuccessful, Grace knew that she had done everything she could to resolve their differences. She walked out of her marriage without shouting accusations or flinging insults. She walked out of her marriage with the certainty that she was honoring her true self with her choice.

Manage thoughts, actions, and reactions

Strong negative emotions mar objectivity because they invite unresolved past injuries into the present moment. Being hurt can spur a number of unconscious choices that act as defenses against further hurt. In the above example involving Grace, her initial reaction to her husband's cheating was name-calling and rage. (The negative ego probably had something to do with this.) Some other common defenses that arise when we are hurt include distancing, not saying hello or good-by, not answering questions, negative facial expressions, giving up, short responses, sarcasm, defeated or angry posture, and anything that resembles a direct or indirect negative reaction to the other person.

As part of the forgiveness process, it's important to expand awareness of our defenses so that we can consciously choose to remove these blocks when they arise. We need to look within at our own thoughts, actions, and reactions. When someone hurts us, what are our tendencies? Have those tendencies caused us more pain or helped us get over the situation more easily? If we find (and we probably will) that we have some negative reactions, that's ok. We can begin today to choose otherwise.

If we've been hurt badly, we might find that our physical bodies still respond negatively to seeing the other person or being in a similar situation. When this is the case, we might find ourselves in a ready-to-battle body position or in a defeated needy stance. Awareness of our reactions is the key. It's normal to continue to react to people who have hurt us. We don't gain from judging ourselves harshly because we can't immediately get over a hurt. As we work on forgiveness, the depth and frequency of our reactions will decrease. Finding compassion in the middle of a negative emotion gets easier and easier with practice.

Think about a time when you got a cut or scrape to your knee. Your body didn't instantly heal. Instead, when physically hurt, our bodies begin a process that heals with time. Healing emotional wounds also takes time. The length of time depends upon the severity of the wound as well as the duration of time that it's been left untreated.

Keep in mind that we can control the thoughts about the event. Grace used the techniques described in Chapter Seven to change the channel whenever she found herself thinking negative thoughts about her husband and his cheating. Whenever she became aware that she was thinking negatively about her husband, Grace chose to replace those negative thoughts with compassion. By giving less air time to the negative, Grace created more space for her own healing.

One common reaction that can occur is the creation of a shadow state. This happens when we make statements like this: "I'll never trust a woman again," or "I'll never ask for help again." As discussed in the chapter on shadow (Chapter Four), trying to avoid pain by embracing an opposite attracts more pain. When examining our thoughts, actions, and reactions, it's a good strategy to make an assessment involving the presence of shadow. This is important because if we allow ourselves to fall into shadow, we will find ourselves with a whole new set of equally frustrating problems in the future. If, after examining our reactions to the event we find shadow energy, we can use the steps described in the shadow chapter to immediately begin balancing that energy.

We do have control over our thoughts, our actions, and our reactions to any event. Being more purposeful and present in our choices empowers our true selves, making the path ahead more clear and negotiable.

Determine personal responsibility

When we are wronged, it's wise to ask ourselves the following: "What can I do to keep that from happening again?" If we recognize measures we could have taken to prevent what happened, then we can take note of the specifics to prevent recurrence. When looking for responsibility, many people will initially respond with a statement like: "Well, if he hadn't done this, then I wouldn't have done that! I can't see how I did anything wrong." This section is not about determining right or wrong or assigning blame or fault.

In Grace's case, she was very aware of her personal responsibility. She recognized that she had overlooked multiple signs of cheating because she didn't want to rock the boat or cause conflict.

Think of Joey. Recall that his wife merely asked to go out as a couple more often. This request ultimately led to the end of his marriage. What can Joey do in the future to keep these kinds of conflicts from happening? Joey can hear the words only; that is, he can stop reading between the lines, or searching for rejection in the choices and statements of others.

Be cautious when looking for personal responsibility. Your goal is to prevent future occurrences, not to assign blame or self-blame. Prevention occurs when specific steps are identified that address contributing factors.

Certainly, there will be times when there is no point in seeking personal responsibility. However, answering the question, "What can I do to keep that from happening again?" can be helpful by providing the true self with a much needed sense of safety.

The purpose of questioning is to prevent recurrence of a negative situation. If we have thoroughly examined a situation, our true selves can relax within the present moment, without unnecessary fears of future harm. This stance further resolves a situation, contributing to the possibility of complete forgiveness.

Bring the feeling of compassion to the person or situation

When we are wronged or hurt, we experience negative feelings. Apologetic words and gestures are often not enough to pull us out of the negative energy associated with the event. Most of the time, this occurs because the hurt has happened within the emotional zone, not the cognitive. To forgive at the feeling level, we can learn to work within it to resolve the emotional pain.

Before we can forgive at the feeling level, however, it's important that we have the ability to summon compassion into a difficult moment. Compassion is the emotional bridge that can lead us out of a difficult and strong emotional state into the powerful and healing presence of forgiveness.

Try this exercise in summoning compassion:

1. Find a quiet place.
2. Think of a cause or a person for whom you feel compassion.
3. Now, think of a person you have a grievance with. (This person you have a grievance with could be yourself!)
4. Turn your attention to the person for whom you feel compassion. Notice how your body experiences the feeling of compassion. As you continue to envision that person deserving of compassion, increase the feeling of compassion with deep breathing—*breathing in* compassion and *breathing out* any discomfort or uncertainty. Take your time and let that feeling of compassion expand throughout your body. Continue breathing deeply and regularly as you gaze upon the image of the person deserving of compassion.
5. Now, filled with compassion, turn your attention to the person or cause with which you have a grievance. Notice the changes in your physical and emotional experience

and begin working immediately to introduce or increase the feeling of compassion. Pay attention to your thoughts. Continue breathing deeply, armed with determination to bring a compassionate response to this person or situation.

6. Be sure to give yourself plenty of time to find the compassion. When you find it, hold it for a while as you gaze upon the image of the person or situation that wronged you.

7. When you have done the best you can, make a decision to reach for compassion anytime thoughts of this person or event arise within you.

In the above exercise, did you notice how the negative feelings dissolved as you deliberately worked to transform the experience? Each time you do this exercise, it gets easier and easier to find compassion.

When you first try this exercise, the odds are that you will experience a drop in your compassionate feelings when you shift your focus to someone with whom you have a grievance. This is expected. Consider yourself fortunate to have an opportunity to forgive—as well as to begin to heal—with compassion. Let's say that, after you found yourself filled with compassion, you imagined a former friend. The supporting thoughts were, "She can't keep her mouth shut. She likes to be in everybody's business," etc. In your search for compassion, remember to separate the deed from the doer and/or to try to find an alternate explanation for the actions. With reference to your friend, consider all the things you do not know about her. Could she be extremely insecure? Who taught her how to get along in a group? What was her childhood like? As you begin to recognize her humanness it gets easier and easier to forgive.

With a working knowledge of how to create a compassionate feeling state, we are ready to heal the emotional wounds at the feeling level. Any time we can reduce negative reactions and feelings toward others, we are helping ourselves heal beyond our own pain.

By working within emotions to forgive, we greatly reduce the negative effects of harm that others have caused. We don't have to wait for something bad to happen to us to practice summoning compassion. The next section presents ideas for how to work on a daily basis to strengthen our compassionate response.

Strengthening our compassionate response

For those of us actively looking for opportunities to strengthen our abilities to find compassion in the moment, a great place to start can be found within our daily activities. We can make summoning compassion a part of our daily routine. Every day, in numerous ways, we have opportunities to link with the emotional feeling of compassion. Reactions may occur that we don't fully understand. People we meet or events that occur can trigger reactions within us that we may not fully understand. We can use those reactions to help us build compassion, to help us heal and to maximize our opportunities to forgive others.

A word of caution: The following example contains about eight opportunities for building compassion or for healing through forgiveness of ourselves or others. The purpose of the example is to demonstrate the number of opportunities that are present, if we just look for them. This is the only purpose. At some point, if we are not careful, we might berate or burden ourselves for having missed so many opportunities. If this works its way into our consciousness, we can immediately stop and replace it with thoughts that congratulate ourselves for working to expand our awareness on our quest to our true selves. If we choose to feel guilty, we are, in actuality, creating another opportunity to build compassion—toward ourselves!

Each potential compassion building opportunity is numbered. A brief discussion of each follows the scenario.

Joe is preparing to leave for work in the morning. He can't find his keys. He's immediately angry and utters a silent remark to himself about his own ineptitude (1). During his search, Joe discovers that his wife used the car and is irritated by the fact that she didn't return the keys to their proper place (2). When he gets ready to leave, his wife offers him a cold and stiff hug at the door (3). Joe mutters good-by without eye contact. In the car, he tunes into the morning radio talk show on the way to work. He says aloud, "That idiot (4), the flaming liberal (5), is on his soapbox again". As he approaches downtown, he notices that same woman, obviously homeless (6), hitting up someone for breakfast money. She's probably a drug addict (7)."

Let's take a closer look:

1. *He can't find his keys. He's immediately angry and utters a silent remark to himself about his own ineptitude.*

   Within this moment, everything is fine until Joe's anger results in a judgment of himself as inept. Instead of opening the door to more negative thoughts, Joe can choose a more compassionate response to himself. At a minimum, he can recognize that he is doing the best he can in each moment. Or he can trust that things are the way they're supposed to be, that is, things happen for a reason, often for reasons that he may never understand.

2. *During his search, Joe discovers that his wife used the car and is irritated by the fact that she didn't put the keys in their proper place.*

   Within the irritation lies the opportunity. It's likely experienced by his wife as criticism. Judgment is at the core of the irritation. Joe also projected his own *ineptitude* onto his wife. Joe can choose a more compassionate response. He can recognize that she's been just as busy as he has. Joe can find understanding and compassion for her. He can do the same for himself.

3. *When he gets ready to leave, his wife offers him a cold and stiff hug at the door.*

Keep in mind that this is Joe's perception of the situation. If he interprets cold and stiff as rejecting, then he has effectively judged his wife as rejecting. Joe has the ability to pull out of this situation. He can search for understanding, evoke compassion, and offer a warm hug with eye contact and a smile. Then, Joe can give himself an inner hug of compassion, congratulating himself for transforming judgment with compassion.

4. *"That idiot..."*
5. *"...the flaming liberal..."*
6. *"...obviously homeless..."*
7. *"Probably a drug addict."*

Name-calling and labeling are clear examples of judgment and hostile thoughts in action. In these examples, Joe is attacking the talk-show host and the woman *based on his perceptions.* He may also be projecting his shadow traits onto these unsuspecting victims. Perhaps by searching within for understanding and generating a compassionate response, he can accept that there are all kinds of folks on this planet each with their own life lessons. His perceptions don't define the talk show host or the woman as wrong or defective. His perceptions define him.

In the above example, there are two key indicators of an opportunity to strengthen compassion. One is the presence of a negative emotion or negative statement. If Joe is looking to strengthen his compassionate response (and ultimately to become a more forgiving person), he can review his day for these two variables—negative emotions or statements.

Also, remember that within our reactions to others we may find an element of shadow. For example, if we have a difficult time feeling compassion for a homeless person, we can search within to find how we are *similar* to the homeless woman or how we are her *opposite.*

Cultural Compassion

In Chapter Two, we discussed the generalizations and judgments that are often present within a culture. In a search for opportunities to heal, we can look within our own culture for its unique set of judgments and generalizations about others. These also represent opportunities to strengthen our compassionate responses. Because we see other groups, cultures, countries, political parties, etc., as separate or different from us, the ground is fertile for judgmental thoughts and ideas.

Often faceless and nameless, the *other* is easy to blame for problems. Whether it's a neighboring country or a neighbor, a compassionate response is activated with the decision to understand the *other* and get to know *those people* (the specific race, the system, the policy, the government, etc.) behind the face. It's easy to maintain distance with a conscious or unconscious choice for a lack of understanding. It's just as easy to take the necessary steps to become acquainted with *those people*, the country, or the ideology that offends us.

Joseph Campbell stated that what we fear (in others) is that which we don't understand. In other words, the more we get to know someone (or the more we know about a situation) the less likely that fear and/or fear-related defenses arise. If we find ourselves caught up in cultural comparisons and judgments, we can recognize the opportunity, stop whatever we are saying, and tell ourselves that we don't have enough information to make those judgments. Just by stopping the flow of negative thoughts, we bring a more compassionate response to the situation.

Forgiving ourselves

The ability to let go of an issue requires self-forgiveness. Until that happens, the situation sits unresolved in the psyche. The more the issue is repressed, the greater the odds that it will be expressed. And, it *will be* expressed regardless of a choice to ignore it. Repressed energy varies in its expression. Sometimes it's a sharp word at an inappropriate moment. Other times it can transform itself into a physical or mental illness. Care and attention to how we treat ourselves is an essential aspect of living a forgiving life.

When I hear clients repeatedly use the phrase, *it's all my fault,* I begin to look for a larger theme of self-blame. The self is ever vigilant to the judgments we make against ourselves, watching and assigning meaning to what it sees and hears. The good news is that we can control what we say to ourselves and we can become more compassionate and forgiving of ourselves from the moment we become aware of the need.

To begin this process, the same basic steps apply that were discussed in the section on forgiving others. There are important distinctions as well as additional steps.

The five steps to self-forgiveness include:

1. Find understanding and compassion for the self.
2. Take necessary actions to resolve any harm toward others or the self.
3. Learn to manage your actions and reactions to the situation.
4. Take steps to avoid recurrence.
5. Bring the feeling of compassion to the person or situation.

Find understanding and compassion for ourselves.

Making a mistake can be humbling. If not handled well within ourselves, making a mistake can also be self-debilitating. Most of us, if we are living, breathing, and human have had times when we have made poor decisions—decisions that have sometimes resulted in hurting ourselves or others. How we process mistakes is important, but we can't mess up too badly if we find understanding and compassion.

In Grace's attempts to grow into her true self, she encountered lots of changes. She mustered courage on multiple occasions to speak her truth (compassionately). While this sounds great after the fact, it doesn't mean it was easy. If she wasn't careful, she would find herself deep into self-criticism. She would wonder if she said it right, if she needed to say more, if she used the wrong tone of voice, if she hurt the other person's feelings, etc. To overcome all of this self-doubt, Grace finally decided that as long as her intention was one of healing or growth, her efforts were worthy—even if she made occasional mistakes. Grace was able to find compassion for herself by separating the deed (perceived mistake) from the doer (her growing, learning compassionate self).

Take necessary actions to resolve any harm toward others or the self.

If we believe we have wronged others, odds are we may not be able to completely forgive ourselves without the extension of an apology or some kind of reparation. While we can't undo a wrong, we do have a choice about what actions we can take as we move forward. Some possible actions are:

- verbal or written apology
- monetary compensation
- performance of an action or service for the person, family, or business harmed

A word of caution: We can benefit by taking care that the action we choose doesn't further aggravate the situation. If the act we propose will cause even more harm, perhaps the time isn't right. Sometimes we want to confess to relieve guilt, but the eventual outcome, especially in relationships, is to place an emotional burden on the other person. Whether a confession contributes to healing is based on individual circumstance.

We harm ourselves physically with attempted suicides, self mutilation, eating disorders, and lack of physical exercise. We harm ourselves emotionally when we're unduly critical of ourselves, neglectful of our own needs, or allow guilt to settle in. Development of healthy *inner parents* can go a long way to prevent harm to ourselves. We allow our *inner mother* expression, when we speak nurturing, guiding, forgiving words to ourselves. We honor our *inner father*, when we take steps that support ourselves and deny harmful choices.

Learn to manage our actions and reactions to the situation.

If we find ourselves ruminating over something we did or said wrong, odds are that the negative ego is unleashed and trying to seize control of our psyches. Think of the impact of hearing a regular barrage of self-blaming self-talk, i.e., *I shouldn't have…, Why didn't I…?, If only…* The unforgiving self (fed by the negative ego's words) reads between the lines, assigning self-deprecating meanings like, "I'm not worthy", "I don't count", or "I'm defective." We must use caution. When we label ourselves negatively, this intensifies our feelings of self-condemnation. Labeling is judging. Our judgments can take on lives of their own by drawing more and more of the same negative energy toward us.

If we find ourselves consumed with negative thoughts of the event, we can use the information from Chapter Seven to control those thoughts and ensure that we don't become consumed with thoughts of the event. If we've realistically assessed the harm that was caused and have begun or completed a plan to address it, we've done all we can. When thoughts of the issue come to mind, we can remind ourselves that we've addressed the issue and then change the channel. Nursing self-blame cripples and victimizes the self.

Some people feel so much self-blame that they contemplate suicide. If you or someone you know is at this point, get help right away. Sometimes we need professional help to reconnect with our true selves. **Suicide is not an option.** Succumbing to despair by choosing suicide causes even more harm to loved ones and/or those who were originally harmed. Suicide is the most violent crime against the self. Equally important, suicide hurts so many others who must now seek resolution without assistance. If you ever seriously consider suicide, don't trust that thought! It represents self-blame, self-pity, or despair that's out of control.

Take steps to avoid recurrence

Prevention of out-of-control self-bashing requires a daily dose of self-empowerment. Harmful behaviors can be reversed. If we've been harming ourselves with negative thoughts, we can create a paragraph or a few easy-to-memorize sentences that carry an enabling message. A well-known example involves a television character who often used an easy to remember catchphrase:

> *I'm good enough, I'm smart enough, and dog-gone it, people like me.*
> —*Al Franken* as *Stuart Smalley* on Saturday Night Live

Often our emotional reactions to others revolve around our own problems with ourselves. Expanding self-awareness and working with forgiveness can resolve these situations and prevent recurrence. Sometimes this work is easier with the support of others. We can ask a friend to hold us accountable. We can contact our church or other support group. When necessary, we can contact a professional counselor.

Bring the feeling of compassion to ourselves

Finding compassion for ourselves requires as much or more work than finding compassion for others. Here's an exercise to try:

1. Find a quiet place. Use whatever method you prefer to become relaxed. Then proceed.
2. Allow an image of yourself and the grievance you have toward yourself to come forward. If you're angry about something you've done, see yourself in that situation. If you have problems with something you've said, see yourself in the act. If the situation occurred at a younger age, see yourself at that age.
3. As you gaze upon this image of yourself, find the words you need to begin to feel compassion toward yourself. Perhaps you need to see that you did the best you could. Recognize

that your childhood wounds may have been at the source
of the problem. Allow yourself to see the image of a young
child taking shape next to the image of yourself.

4. Filled with compassion, in your mind's eye, embrace these
    aspects of yourself. Allow the feeling of compassion to exude
    from your body toward these wounded parts of yourself. Extend
    this healing moment as long as is comfortable for you.

5. When you're ready, allow the images to dissolve, then
    open your eyes with the awareness that you can call upon
    compassion whenever negative thoughts or feelings arise.

Dealing with guilt

One way to unearth self-forgiveness opportunities is to think
about the things we have guilt about. Guilt does have a positive
purpose when used wisely. Guilt is not to be a means of constant self-
belittlement. Instead, when feelings of guilt arise, we are being made
aware of a situation in which we are violating an internal standard.
Once we're aware, we can identify and take corrective action. The
corrective action helps us maintain integrity with ourselves.

If it's too late to correct a situation, applying the lesson learned to
present relationships and situations can be the corrective action. For
example, if we feel guilty for not showing appreciation to an elderly
relative before their death, we can determine to show appreciation as
situations occur with our living relatives. When guilt arises, we can
say to ourselves: *I've taken steps to prevent that from happening again.*

If we want to stay focused on our quest to our true selves, a
necessary step is to rid ourselves of the often heavy burden of guilt.
One way to deal with old guilt is to make a list of the things that we
have guilt about. With that list in hand, we can review the five steps
of self-forgiveness to locate any possible actions. This may take more
than a one-time sitting. Odds are we won't remember every action
(or inaction) that we feel guilt about. To completely work through
past guilt, we can resolve to watch for and address guilty feelings
when they arise. A small notebook or handy slip of paper carried
throughout the day help us record these incidents. As we recognize
the presence of guilt or other opportunities to increase understanding

and compassion, we can write them down to ensure that we complete the work later in the day. As our list grows, it's likely that just two or three recurring themes are fueling them. When we discover these themes, we can narrow our focus as we work on our core issues.

As we work through our guilt repertoire, an essential step to consider is whether the guilt is justified. For example, if we have guilt about not telling our parents to talk nicer to each other, we must ask ourselves if it was our responsibility to do so. Furthermore, is it reasonable to believe that we are to respond to all injustices we observe just because we are aware of them? Relieving ourselves of the guilt of events that are not our responsibility is very freeing.

Deliberate forgiveness

Doing the work of forgiveness and self-forgiveness culminates in more present-moment awareness and present-moment compassion. We will find that we are likely to catch (and stop) ourselves in the middle of a negative thought or emotion during an interaction with someone. We become more self-aware. We are being more in-the-moment (as opposed to reacting to the past). We are practicing very healthy self-control when we stop ourselves from saying something we don't mean. There is tremendous power in being in command of the moment.

Here is something that we can try when we catch ourselves in the middle of a negative thought or emotion in the moment…

1. Acknowledge the negative feeling as possibly having ties to negative, unresolved events or thoughts in the past.
2. Make a mental note to revisit this moment or issue later in the day during deliberate work on forgiveness.
3. To diffuse or reverse our feelings *in that moment*, we can disconnect somewhat by saying to ourselves: *Isn't this interesting that I am reacting this way?*
4. Later in the day, during our deliberate forgiveness time, we can revisit the situations and the reaction that occurred by deliberately bringing up an image of the event or person.
5. At this point, we can ask ourselves: *How does this moment, this person, or this event relate to something in my past?*

6. Allow a memory to come forward; you may see a time when you were in a similar situation. Or you may see yourself as a young child, hurting, wanting love or feeling disregarded. If so, add an image of you as a young child to this exercise. (It's ok if nothing from the past comes forward).

7. Search for compassion for yourself and the other person. In your mind's eye, send feelings of compassion with your eyes and from your heart-center.

8. Envision embracing all parties allowing the feeling of compassion to surround and connect you.

9. When you're ready, allow the image to dissolve.

10. Give yourself an inner hug, and congratulate yourself for your commitment to personal and spiritual growth.

One part of my nightly routine is to take the time to review the day for forgiveness opportunities and practice deliberate forgiveness. The key to success is awareness of negative emotions that occur during the day and the ability to recall them. To ensure balance, I also review my day for times when I was fully engaged in-the-moment. It's a rare day that I don't have anything to work on. As time has passed, my review finds that I am more in-the-moment than not. This single exercise has brought me a tremendous amount of peace while serving to give me greater command and enjoyment of the present moment. I highly recommend it.

The benefits of forgiveness

The beauty of forgiveness can be found in its healing nature. Forgiveness clears up perception. Forgiveness helps us to see our friends and family for who they really are, not as extensions of our unresolved emotional issues. Forgiveness contributes to others' healing by keeping interactions in the present moment. With forgiveness, intimacy in relationships grows exponentially, with all parties benefiting.

Forgiveness opens the way for rewards like an enhanced sense of inner peace, greater self-expression, improved physical health, and an expanded capacity to live and operate in the moment.

Forgiveness and how to heal and empower the true self

Forgiveness is an incredibly effective tool for moving beyond childhood hurts and present-moment difficulties. Using forgiveness tools and strengthening a compassionate response helps to maintain a healthy *self-concept* by keeping past hurts out of the present moment. Furthermore, awareness of old, unhealed wounds is expanded creating an opportunity for healing. Forgiveness, whether extended toward others or ourselves, is a healthy *coping skill* that assists in the maintenance of healthy *relationships*.

Forgiveness heals and empowers the self by making space for self-awareness, self-love, and self-expression. Forgiveness heals!

This chapter has detailed forgiveness and compassion-strengthening strategies. The following exercise may be helpful in stimulating your thinking with regard to your experience.

Exercise: Consider the following questions:
1. Practice the forgiveness steps. Think of someone or some situation that you would like to forgive.
   a. Find understanding and compassion by thinking of an alternate explanation for what occurred, i.e., an explanation that invites compassion.
   b. Think again of the person who needs forgiving. Remind yourself of the wrong that has occurred. Reduce the negative emotions or physical feelings by *changing the channel* or repeating the alternate explanation for what occurred.
   c. Think about your role, if any, in the situation. What can you do to prevent this type of situation from occurring again?
   d. Practice bringing the feeling of compassion to that person and/or event.
2. Reflect on any generalizations and judgments present in the cultures and subcultures that surround you. Pick one issue/person with whom to work. Research to learn more about it.
3. Practice the self-forgiveness steps. Think of something for which you would like self-forgiveness.

    a. Find understanding and compassion for yourself by accepting that you made a mistake. Mistakes are part of human existence.

    b. If you have not taken any action to resolve the harm, make a plan to do so. Include dates and specific actions.

    c. Manage your actions and reactions by controlling your thoughts about the event, person, or situation.

    d. Ask yourself what you can do to prevent this type of situation from occurring again.

    e. Practice bringing the feeling of compassion to yourself.

4. Think of something that irritated you recently. Apply the deliberate forgiveness steps to that situation.

5. Now that you've practiced forgiveness and self-forgiveness, think about how these ideas can enhance your self-concept, improve your coping, and maintain healthier relationships.

Let us not regret the past. Let us not worry about the future. Go back to the present moment and live deeply the present moment. Because the present moment is the only moment where you can touch life. Life is available only in the present moment.

—Thich Nhat Hanh, *Resting in the River*,
Shambhala Sun,
March 1998.

Chapter 11 – The Present Moment

It's been about thirty years since I was introduced to the idea of being *in the moment*. I recall thinking that the whole concept was a cool idea but I couldn't quite understand how to apply it. So I forgot about the issue, setting it aside for consideration at some unknown future time.

The issue resurfaced for me about 18 years later when Maggie, a friend of mine now deceased, included me in a group discussion that involved my very first shadow exercise. I remember sitting in a living room with a group of like-minded women, considering all the implications of having a shadow and working with my shadow traits. Listening to Maggie, her excitement, her desire to share this information, I knew she was on to something. I learned that night that this thing called *shadow* could interfere with my present moment, but I still didn't have the tools or information I needed to regain control of my moment. As I had done eighteen years earlier, I set the issue aside for future consideration.

Two years later, I began working with clients in private practice. With each new client, my understanding of present-moment-living expanded. I came to recognize how much of the past we bring into the present. I worked side by side with my clients, dissecting past pain from present-moment perceptions. At the same time, my own understanding of how my past was in my present grew exponentially. This time, however, I didn't set the issue aside. I wanted more than just awareness. I wanted something to *do* to get the unhealthy past out of my present. Thus began the work that has culminated in the publication of this book.

The strategies detailed in this book follow the general strategy I use in counseling. I work with my clients to expand their awareness of how childhood pain and difficult experiences can negatively interfere with the present moment (Part One). We examine present day experiences (dreams, emotions, shadow, etc.) for clues of how past pain is expressed in the present (Part Two). Armed with awareness, we begin testing strategies for healing and staying fully present (Part Three).

Over time, I've witnessed the power of this approach. I've been humbled by the courage and determination of others to embrace this work. I've witnessed the power of the true self within others as it finds expression and gains command of the moment.

To you, the reader, I offer these ideas for your consideration. I recognize that the number of questions, strategies, and ideas to consider might at first appear overwhelming. The ideas and strategies are presented in a certain order but using that order is not required. Healing and connecting with the true self begins with the choice to seize and act upon just *one single strategy or idea*. If one idea is more appealing than another, start there. When that one feels complete, go to the next. Awareness expands as the work is continued. Awareness opens up avenues to try additional strategies.

The point is to begin. Don't wait until tomorrow. Start now. In this moment, you have a choice. Choose wisely.

Your true self awaits...

A gift for you!

I have recorded some meditations that can be helpful to you on your journey to discover and empower your True Self.

The meditations are available to those who purchase this book to download free of charge from: www.howdoifindme.com

To access the audio download, you'll need a user name and password

Enter the user name: ireadthebook
Enter the password: trueself

I plan to continue to add meditations and/or other audio that supports the information in this book. Be sure to check the website regularly for updates.

Questions and comments are welcome via the following e-mail address:

mkillgore@gmail.com

Bibliography

The following books have played a significant role in the conceptualization of the ideas in this book. They each contain core truths that can dramatically support discovery and empowerment of the True Self.

Bradshaw, John. *Healing The Shame That Binds You.* Florida: Health Communications, Inc., 1988.

Branden, Nathaniel. *The Six Pillars of Self-Esteem.* New York: Bantam Books, 1994.

Dyer, Wayne. *Your Erroneous Zones.* New York: HarperCollins Publishers. 1976.

Hay, Louise. *You Can Heal Your Life,* California: Hay House, 1984

Johnson, Robert A. & Ruhl, Jerry M. *Balancing Heaven and Earth: A Memoir.* New York: HarperCollins Publishers, 1998.

Johnson, Robert A. *Inner Work.* New York: HarperCollins Publishers. 1986.

Johnson, Robert A. *Owning Your Own Shadow: Understanding the Dark Side of the Psyche.* New York: HarperCollins Publishers, 1991.

Jung, C. G. *Man and His Symbols.* New York: Doubleday, 1964.

Jung, C.G. *Memories, Dreams and Reflections.* New York: Random House, 1961.

Jung, C.G. *Modern Man In Search of a Soul.* Florida: Harcourt, Inc., 1933.

Moore, Thomas. *Care of the Soul.* New York: Harper Collins Publishers, 1984.

Myss, Carolyn, Ph.D. *Anatomy of the Spirit.* New York: Three Rivers Press, 1996.

Peck, M. Scott, M.D. *The Road Less Traveled.* New York: Simon & Schuster, 1978.

Satir, Virginia. *Conjoint Family Therapy: Your Many Faces.* Palo Alto, California: Science and Behavior Books, 1983.

Zimberoff, Diane. *Breaking Free from the Victim Trap.* Issaquah, Washington: Wellness Press, 1989.

Made in the USA